SUZANNE BYRD

Hidden Rituals

Breaking Free from OCD as a Woman

First published by Mental Health Publishing 2025

Copyright © 2025 by Suzanne Byrd

All rights reserved. No part of this publication may be reproduced, stored or transmitted in any form or by any means, electronic, mechanical, photocopying, recording, scanning, or otherwise without written permission from the publisher. It is illegal to copy this book, post it to a website, or distribute it by any other means without permission.

First edition

This book was professionally typeset on Reedsy.
Find out more at reedsy.com

Contents

1	Understanding OCD in Women	1
2	The Spectrum of OCD – Beyond the Stereotypes	8
3	The Role of Perfectionism in Women's OCD	17
4	Unraveling "Pure O" and Intrusive Thoughts	27
5	Beyond Rituals – The Emotional Cost of OCD	36
6	The Hidden Battle – OCD and Motherhood	45
7	The Impact of Relationships and Social Expectations	54
8	The Road to Recovery – Introduction to Cognitive-Behavioral...	63
9	Step-by-Step: Crafting Your Personal CBT Plan	71
10	Breaking the Cycle – Exposure and Response Prevention in...	82
11	Sustaining Recovery – Building Resilience and Self-Care...	91
12	Living Beyond OCD – Empowerment, Advocacy, and the Future	101

1

Understanding OCD in Women

Obsessive-compulsive disorder (OCD) is a condition that many understand only in its most stereotypical form—a relentless cycle of intrusive thoughts followed by compulsive actions. However, for women, OCD often carries an extra layer of complexity. This chapter lays the groundwork for understanding the unique ways in which OCD manifests in women, challenging common myths, and setting the stage for a journey toward recovery and self-empowerment.

Defining OCD and Its Unique Impact on Women

OCD is a mental health disorder characterized by persistent, unwanted thoughts (obsessions) and repetitive behaviors (compulsions) that a person feels compelled to perform. While anyone can experience these symptoms, women often encounter a distinct set of challenges. From the pressure of perfectionism to the emotional strain of balancing personal and societal expectations, the manifestations of OCD in women can be both subtle and profound.

For many women, the experience of OCD is intertwined with the expectations placed upon them from a young age. Society often holds women to high standards of care, beauty, and behavior, and these pressures can intensify the internal dialogue of doubt and anxiety. In many cases, the obsessive thoughts are not merely random intrusions but are linked to a deep-seated fear of not meeting these expectations. Whether it's an overwhelming need for perfection in work, appearance, or parenting, OCD in women frequently finds fertile ground in the realm of self-imposed high standards.

The Invisible Struggle: Beyond Stereotypes

There is a common misconception that OCD is simply about cleanliness or organizing things in a specific order. In reality, OCD is far more complex and multifaceted. For many women, the intrusive thoughts do not always align with the traditional image of "washing hands repeatedly" or "checking doors." Instead, these obsessions can be of a deeply personal nature—ranging from doubts about one's worth as a mother or partner to relentless concerns about personal safety and morality.

One underrecognized aspect is what is often referred to as "pure O," a term used to describe OCD that manifests without overt compulsions. Women suffering from "pure O" might experience a barrage of intrusive thoughts—such as fears of harming a loved one or doubts about one's moral integrity—without engaging in visible rituals. This internalized battle can leave many women feeling isolated and misunderstood, as their struggle is not immediately apparent to others.

Moreover, women may experience OCD differently during various stages of life. For example, hormonal fluctuations can exacerbate symptoms, making the disorder particularly challenging during menstruation, pregnancy, or menopause. The added stressors of these periods, combined with societal expectations, can create a perfect storm where intrusive thoughts and compulsive behaviors become more pronounced.

The Role of Perfectionism and Societal Pressure

Perfectionism is often at the heart of OCD in women. From an early age, many girls are taught that perfection is not just desirable—it is necessary. The drive to excel in every aspect of life, whether in academics, career, relationships, or appearance, can set an unattainable standard that fuels obsessive thoughts. When perfectionism becomes a daily burden, the mind can become trapped in a cycle of self-criticism and anxiety, with even minor deviations from an ideal being perceived as catastrophic failures.

For instance, a woman who is a high achiever in her career might find herself obsessing over a single mistake in a presentation, magnifying the error in her mind until it feels insurmountable. Similarly, a mother might constantly worry about whether her parenting decisions are "right" or "enough," even when her children are thriving. These examples underscore how perfectionism can be both a motivator and a source of deep distress. It is the gap between the ideal and the real that becomes the breeding ground for OCD.

Societal messages that dictate how women should behave and appear add another layer of pressure. Advertisements, media portrayals, and even well-meaning advice from friends and family can reinforce the notion that any deviation from the norm is a sign of personal failure. This external pressure often merges with internal standards, making it difficult for women to distinguish between healthy striving for excellence and the paralyzing grip of OCD.

Dispelling Myths and Recognizing Realities

One of the primary hurdles in understanding OCD in women is the proliferation of myths and misconceptions about the disorder. Many still believe that OCD is a quirky habit rather than a serious mental health condition. Such misunderstandings can be especially damaging to women, who may already be grappling with feelings of inadequacy and self-doubt.

A common myth is that those with OCD simply need to "snap out of it" or "try harder" to control their thoughts. This oversimplification ignores the complexity of the disorder. OCD is not a failure of willpower—it is a neurological condition that involves imbalances in brain chemistry and neural circuitry. For many women, the stigma surrounding mental health can prevent them from seeking the help they need, exacerbating the cycle of shame and isolation.

It is crucial to acknowledge that the experience of OCD is as diverse as the women who live with it. While some may exhibit obvious compulsions, others struggle silently with intrusive thoughts that leave them feeling alienated from their own identities. Recognizing this diversity is the first step toward breaking down the barriers of stigma and misunderstanding.

The Intersection of OCD and Identity

OCD often intertwines with a woman's sense of identity, impacting how she perceives herself and her place in the world. The relentless internal dialogue of doubt and self-criticism can erode self-esteem, making it difficult to see one's strengths and accomplishments. For many women, OCD becomes an unwanted part of their identity—an invisible label that colors every aspect of their lives.

Consider the case of a woman who has dedicated her life to caring for her family, only to be haunted by intrusive thoughts that undermine her confidence as a nurturer. She may begin to question every decision she makes, worrying that any misstep could harm those she loves. Over time, these doubts can become so pervasive that they overshadow her genuine achievements and positive qualities. In such cases, OCD is not just a set of symptoms—it becomes a lens through which every aspect of life is scrutinized and devalued.

Understanding OCD in women, therefore, requires a compassionate examination of how the disorder interacts with self-identity. It is about recognizing that the intrusive thoughts and compulsive behaviors are not reflections of a woman's character or worth, but rather symptoms of a complex mental health condition that deserves understanding and treatment.

The Journey Toward Empowerment

While the challenges of OCD can feel overwhelming, it is important to remember that recovery is not only possible—it is within reach. This book is dedicated to providing a roadmap for women who are ready to break free from the grip of OCD and reclaim their lives. By combining clinical insights with cognitive-behavioral techniques (CBT) and heartfelt case studies, we aim to offer practical tools that empower women to challenge and overcome their intrusive thoughts.

One of the key components of this journey is education. By learning about the nature of OCD, understanding its triggers, and debunking the myths that surround it, women can begin to separate themselves from the disorder. This separation is essential for building a sense of identity that is not defined by anxiety or compulsive rituals.

Another important aspect is self-compassion. Women with OCD often hold themselves to impossibly high standards, and this self-imposed pressure can be a significant barrier to recovery. Cultivating self-compassion means recognizing that mistakes and imperfections are a natural part of being human. It involves treating oneself with the same kindness and understanding that one would offer a dear friend.

In practical terms, cognitive-behavioral therapy provides actionable strategies to disrupt the cycle of OCD. Techniques such as exposure and response prevention (ERP) empower individuals to face their fears head-on, gradually diminishing the power of intrusive thoughts. Through small, deliberate steps, women can learn to challenge the irrational beliefs that fuel their anxiety, replacing them with more balanced, realistic perspectives.

Looking Ahead

As we embark on this exploration of OCD in women, it is important to acknowledge that each woman's journey is unique. The strategies and techniques presented in this book are meant to serve as a foundation—a starting point from which readers can build their own personalized approach to recovery. The chapters that follow will delve deeper into the various facets of OCD, from the insidious nature of "pure O" to the specific challenges of postpartum OCD. We will also explore the powerful role of cognitive-behavioral techniques and the inspiring stories of women who have successfully navigated their way out of the darkness.

This chapter has set the stage by offering a broad yet detailed understanding of OCD as it affects women. It has challenged the myths that have long clouded public perception and has highlighted the unique pressures that can amplify the symptoms of this disorder. Most importantly, it has established the belief that knowledge, self-compassion, and practical strategies can pave the way to recovery.

For women who have felt isolated by their experiences or misunderstood by those around them, this book is a reminder that you are not alone. The journey toward breaking free from OCD is not a straight path—

it is a winding road filled with setbacks, breakthroughs, and moments of profound self-discovery. Each step you take is a testament to your strength, resilience, and commitment to reclaiming your life.

As we move forward, remember that understanding is the first step toward change. By recognizing the intricate ways in which OCD intertwines with the pressures and expectations placed upon women, we can begin to dismantle its hold. Through informed strategies, heartfelt stories, and practical tools, this book invites you to take that courageous step toward healing—one small, empowering move at a time.

In the chapters that follow, we will explore in greater detail the specific manifestations of OCD in women, the cognitive-behavioral techniques that have proven effective, and the real-life stories of women who have found hope and recovery. This comprehensive approach is designed to help you navigate the complexities of OCD, offering not only insights but also practical steps for a brighter, freer future.

By embracing both knowledge and compassion, you are taking the first vital step toward a life where OCD no longer defines you. Welcome to your journey of transformation—welcome to a future where you can break free from the hidden rituals that have held you captive for too long.

2

The Spectrum of OCD – Beyond the Stereotypes

Obsessive-compulsive disorder is far more nuanced than the tidy image many have of excessive cleaning or incessant checking. In this chapter, we explore the broad spectrum of OCD manifestations, emphasizing that there is no one-size-fits-all experience. For many women, OCD is a silent struggle that extends well beyond stereotypical compulsions. By understanding the diversity of symptoms—from the subtle to the overt—we can begin to see how deeply personal this condition is and why a tailored approach to treatment and recovery is so essential.

The Many Faces of OCD

When most people think of OCD, the first images that come to mind are those of individuals repeatedly washing their hands or organizing objects in a precise order. While these behaviors are common, they represent only a fraction of the ways OCD can present itself. For many women, the intrusive thoughts and anxiety can take on forms that are not immediately visible to others.

Beyond Cleaning and Checking

The classical image of OCD often involves repetitive cleaning or checking behaviors. However, many women experience what is known as "mental rituals" or "pure O," where the compulsions are not physical actions but internal processes. These mental rituals might include silently repeating phrases, mentally reviewing events to check for mistakes, or overanalyzing one's thoughts and decisions. The absence of overt behavior often makes these symptoms harder for others to recognize, leaving many women feeling isolated in their experience.

Intrusive Thoughts and Mental Rituals

Intrusive thoughts are a central element of OCD, and they can be both distressing and persistent. Women may experience thoughts that are violent, taboo, or contrary to their deeply held values. These thoughts are not indicative of a person's character but are rather a manifestation of the disorder. For example, a woman might have intrusive thoughts about harming a loved one or making a critical mistake at work—even though these thoughts are completely unwanted and repulsive to her. The accompanying mental rituals can involve endless internal debates, repeated self-reassurance, or ruminating over the potential consequences of these thoughts.

The Internal Battle

For many, the struggle with OCD is an internal war fought in silence. While external compulsions can be observed and understood, internal obsessions—such as overwhelming doubts or irrational fears—remain hidden. This can lead to a double burden: not only is the individual battling distressing thoughts, but she is also burdened with the guilt and shame of those thoughts. The internal battle is often fought in solitude, making it even more challenging to seek help or receive understanding from those around her.

The Unique Experience of Women

Women often experience OCD in ways that are influenced by a complex interplay of biological, social, and cultural factors. These influences can shape both the content of the intrusive thoughts and the nature of the compulsive behaviors.

Biological and Hormonal Influences

Research suggests that hormonal fluctuations can significantly affect the intensity and frequency of OCD symptoms in women. Phases such as menstruation, pregnancy, and menopause bring about changes in hormone levels that may exacerbate existing symptoms or trigger new episodes of intrusive thoughts and compulsions. For instance, many women report an increase in anxiety and obsessive thoughts during the premenstrual phase, when the body's chemistry is in flux. Similarly, the postpartum period can be particularly challenging, as the dramatic hormonal shifts and new responsibilities converge to heighten anxiety and intrusive thoughts.

Social Expectations and Gender Roles

Social conditioning plays a pivotal role in shaping how OCD manifests in women. From an early age, girls are often encouraged to be meticulous, caring, and self-sacrificing. These expectations can inadvertently foster an environment where obsessive thoughts about perfection and responsibility thrive. A woman might obsess over whether she is being a "good enough" mother, partner, or professional, constantly scrutinizing her actions against an ideal that is virtually impossible to achieve. The pressure to meet these high standards can intensify the inner turmoil associated with OCD, as any deviation from the ideal is magnified in her mind.

The Duality of Visibility

OCD in women is characterized by a duality of visibility. On one hand, certain compulsions—such as repeated checking or cleaning—are visible to others and may attract unwanted attention or judgment. On the other hand, the more subtle aspects of the disorder, such as mental rituals and internal obsessions, remain hidden. This dichotomy can lead to a sense of isolation; while a woman might appear composed on the outside, she could be grappling with relentless internal chaos. The invisibility of these struggles often means that the severity of her condition is underestimated by friends, family, or even healthcare providers.

Personal Narratives and Case Examples

To truly understand the spectrum of OCD, it is essential to listen to the voices of those who experience it daily. Consider the story of Elena, a professional in her early thirties who was known for her impeccable organizational skills and calm demeanor. On the surface, Elena's life seemed to be in perfect order. Yet beneath that facade, she was locked in a perpetual cycle of doubt and anxiety. Elena's OCD did not involve any overt compulsions like excessive cleaning; instead, her mind was consumed by intrusive doubts about every decision she made—be it at work or in her personal life. Every error, no matter how minor, was magnified into a catastrophe in her internal narrative. Over time, Elena's internal struggle began to affect her relationships and her work, leading her to seek therapy where she eventually learned to differentiate between healthy self-reflection and the destructive patterns of OCD.

Another case is that of Maria, a new mother who found herself overwhelmed by intrusive thoughts shortly after giving birth. Maria's thoughts were filled with doubts about her ability to care for her newborn—thoughts that were entirely at odds with her loving nature. The invisible torment of questioning every action and fearing the worst led her to feel isolated, even as those around her celebrated her new role. It was only when Maria began to explore the underlying mechanisms of her OCD that she could start to see her condition as a manageable disorder rather than a personal failing. Through therapy and support groups, she learned that many women experience similar challenges, and that her thoughts were not a reflection of her competence as a mother but symptoms of a larger, treatable condition.

These personal narratives highlight the vast diversity in how OCD manifests. They illustrate that the disorder is not defined solely by visible behaviors but also by the internal experiences that can be just as, if not more, debilitating.

Challenging Stereotypes and Expanding Awareness

One of the most significant barriers to effective treatment for OCD in women is the persistence of stereotypes. The narrow depiction of OCD as simply a set of quirky habits not only trivializes the disorder but also discourages those affected from seeking help. It is crucial to challenge these misconceptions and raise awareness about the true nature of OCD.

Redefining OCD

Rather than being seen as a collection of eccentric behaviors, OCD should be recognized as a complex and multifaceted mental health condition that affects every aspect of a person's life. For women, the disorder is intertwined with issues of identity, self-worth, and societal expectations. By broadening the understanding of OCD, we can create a more empathetic and effective approach to treatment—one that addresses both the visible compulsions and the hidden internal struggles.

The Impact of Misconceptions

Misconceptions about OCD can lead to delays in diagnosis and treatment. When symptoms are minimized or misinterpreted as mere quirks, women may internalize the stigma and feel ashamed of their struggles. This can prevent them from seeking the help they need and prolong the suffering caused by the disorder. Educating the public, as well as healthcare professionals, about the diverse presentations of OCD is a critical step toward ensuring that more women receive timely and effective support.

Building a Broader Support System

Understanding that OCD exists on a spectrum helps foster a more inclusive support system. It encourages the development of tailored therapeutic interventions that consider both the overt and covert manifestations of the disorder. Peer support groups, for example, can be invaluable for women who feel isolated by their symptoms. Sharing experiences with others who understand the nuances of OCD can validate their feelings and provide hope. In these communities, women learn that they are not alone in their struggles and that recovery is possible through a combination of professional guidance, self-help techniques, and mutual support.

Embracing a Holistic Approach to Treatment

Given the wide spectrum of OCD symptoms, particularly as experienced by women, treatment must be equally multifaceted. A holistic approach to therapy is essential—one that addresses the biological, psychological, and social dimensions of the disorder.

Cognitive-Behavioral Therapy and Beyond

Cognitive-behavioral therapy (CBT) remains one of the most effective treatments for OCD. However, for many women, combining CBT with other therapeutic approaches can lead to even more comprehensive care. Techniques such as mindfulness meditation, acceptance and commitment therapy (ACT), and even pharmacotherapy can complement traditional CBT, offering additional tools to manage both the intrusive thoughts and the underlying emotional distress.

Personalized Treatment Plans

Every woman's experience with OCD is unique, and treatment should be tailored to her specific needs. Personalized treatment plans that take into account the severity of symptoms, the presence of co-occurring conditions such as anxiety or depression, and the impact of hormonal changes are critical. For instance, a woman experiencing a surge in symptoms during her menstrual cycle may benefit from strategies that specifically address hormonal influences on mood and cognition. Similarly, a new mother dealing with postpartum OCD might find it helpful to incorporate parenting support and stress management techniques into her overall treatment plan.

The Role of Self-Advocacy

Empowering women to advocate for their own mental health is a vital part of the recovery process. This involves learning to recognize when symptoms are a manifestation of OCD rather than personal shortcomings. Self-advocacy also means communicating openly with healthcare providers, family members, and support networks about the realities of living with OCD. By challenging stereotypes and asserting their needs, women can help shift the conversation around OCD from one of stigma to one of understanding and empowerment.

Looking Ahead

As we continue this exploration of OCD, it becomes clear that understanding the spectrum of symptoms is the first step toward effective intervention and recovery. In the next chapters, we will delve deeper into specific aspects of OCD—such as the role of perfectionism, the intricacies of "pure O," and the unique challenges faced by mothers. Each subsequent chapter will build on the foundation laid here, offering practical cognitive-behavioral strategies and real-life examples to guide you on your journey to healing.

Recognizing the diversity of OCD experiences is not just an academic exercise; it is a call to action. It is an invitation to challenge the narrow stereotypes that have long confined our understanding of the disorder and to embrace a more inclusive view that acknowledges the complex realities of women's lives. Whether your struggles are visible to the outside world or hidden behind a veil of internal turmoil, know that every aspect of your experience matters. The full spectrum of OCD is not a weakness—it is a reflection of the multifaceted nature of human emotion and thought.

In embracing this broader perspective, we pave the way for more compassionate treatment approaches and a deeper societal understanding of mental health. By shedding light on the hidden facets of OCD, especially those that disproportionately affect women, we begin to dismantle the barriers that have kept so many in silence for far too long.

This chapter has sought to broaden your understanding of OCD by exploring its varied manifestations and highlighting the importance of individualized care. It is a reminder that while OCD may present in many forms, the journey toward recovery is unified by the common goal of reclaiming control over one's life and identity. With each subsequent chapter, we will continue to explore practical strategies and inspiring stories that illustrate the path from isolation to empowerment.

As you reflect on the information presented here, consider how this broadened perspective on OCD might change the way you see your own experiences or those of the women around you. Recognizing that OCD is not a monolithic condition but a spectrum of challenges and experiences is a powerful step toward fostering empathy, understanding, and effective treatment. In doing so, we open the door to a future where every woman can break free from the hidden rituals that have held her back and step into a life defined by resilience, self-compassion, and hope.

Welcome to the next phase of your journey—a journey that acknowledges every facet of your struggle and offers a path toward comprehensive healing.

3

The Role of Perfectionism in Women's OCD

Perfectionism is a powerful and pervasive force that shapes the inner world of many women with OCD. In this chapter, we will delve deep into how perfectionism not only fuels obsessive-compulsive behaviors but also intertwines with societal expectations, self-identity, and emotional wellbeing. By understanding this relationship, readers can gain insights into the origins of their struggles and learn strategies to break free from the cycle of unattainable standards and self-criticism.

The Perfectionism Paradox

At its core, perfectionism is the belief that one must be flawless in every aspect of life—whether in personal appearance, professional performance, or even interpersonal relationships. For many women with OCD, this belief becomes a double-edged sword. On one hand, striving for excellence can motivate growth and achievement. On the other, it creates an environment where every mistake or perceived shortcoming is magnified into a catastrophic failure. This relentless pursuit of perfection not only drives obsessive thoughts but also reinforces a cycle of compulsive behaviors aimed at "fixing" or preventing imperfections.

Women with OCD often experience a constant internal dialogue that scrutinizes every decision and action. Even when they achieve success, the nagging voice of self-doubt can turn triumph into an opportunity for further criticism. This inner critic is relentless, ensuring that nothing ever feels quite "good enough." The paradox of perfectionism lies in the fact that while the pursuit of flawlessness is intended to protect and improve self-worth, it ultimately undermines confidence and creates additional layers of anxiety and self-reproach.

The Roots of Perfectionism in Women

Societal Influences and Cultural Norms

From a young age, many girls are taught to value perfection. Cultural narratives often idealize the image of a perfect daughter, student, friend, and eventually, a perfect professional, partner, and mother. These messages are reinforced by media portrayals, educational expectations, and even well-meaning advice from family and peers. For instance, the pressure to excel academically and later to juggle the demands of a career and home life can set an incredibly high standard that few can realistically achieve.

These societal pressures are compounded by the expectation that women should be nurturing, patient, and self-sacrificing. As a result, any deviation from these ideals is seen not as a natural human error but as a personal failing. The constant comparison to an idealized image fosters an environment where perfectionism becomes a default mindset—a standard that must be met at all costs.

Early Experiences and Family Dynamics

Family dynamics also play a significant role in shaping perfectionistic tendencies. Many women with OCD recall childhood environments where achievements were highly praised and mistakes were harshly criticized. Whether it was receiving accolades for perfect grades or being reprimanded for a misstep, these early experiences can plant the seeds of perfectionism. When a child learns that love, approval, or success is conditional on flawless performance, the natural outcome is an internalized pressure to be perfect in order to be worthy.

These ingrained messages can persist into adulthood, where every decision is measured against the impossible standard set during those formative years. For women with OCD, this often manifests as a perpetual cycle of self-monitoring and compulsive behavior, where every action is scrutinized to avoid any hint of imperfection.

How Perfectionism Fuels OCD

The Cycle of Obsessive Doubt

At the heart of OCD lies an overwhelming sense of doubt—a persistent uncertainty about one's actions, decisions, or even thoughts. When perfectionism is added to the mix, this doubt is intensified. The mind begins to obsess over every minor detail, constantly questioning whether a mistake has been made or if something essential has been overlooked. This obsessive doubt is not limited to external tasks; it permeates every facet of life, from professional responsibilities to personal relationships.

For example, consider a woman who is responsible for organizing a family event. The pressure to have every detail planned to perfection can trigger a cascade of intrusive thoughts: "Did I miss an important detail? Is everything arranged in the perfect order? What if someone criticizes my efforts?" In an effort to quell these doubts, she may engage in repetitive checking or over-preparation, both of which are common compulsions in OCD. The result is a never-ending loop where the need for certainty leads to behaviors that only serve to reinforce the obsessive cycle.

The Emotional Toll of Perfectionism

The emotional consequences of perfectionism are profound. Constantly striving for an unattainable ideal can lead to chronic stress, anxiety, and feelings of inadequacy. Women with OCD may find that their self-worth is inextricably linked to their ability to meet these high standards. When perfection is not achieved—an inevitability in the human experience—the outcome is intense self-criticism and disappointment.

This emotional toll often manifests as a pervasive sense of failure. Even when achievements are celebrated, the focus remains on the next challenge, and the momentary relief is quickly replaced by renewed anxiety over future shortcomings. This relentless pressure can also contribute to the development of co-occurring conditions such as depression and generalized anxiety disorder, further complicating the path to recovery.

Cognitive Distortions and All-or-Nothing Thinking

Perfectionism in OCD is closely linked to cognitive distortions—irrational and often harmful patterns of thinking. One of the most common distortions is all-or-nothing thinking, where situations are viewed in black-and-white terms. A single mistake is seen as evidence of complete failure, and even minor imperfections are magnified to catastrophic proportions. This binary way of thinking not only intensifies obsessive thoughts but also drives the compulsive behaviors aimed at avoiding any deviation from perfection.

For instance, a woman may believe that if she does not execute a task flawlessly, she is inherently flawed or unworthy. This belief leads to extreme anxiety and an unyielding compulsion to perform tasks repeatedly until they meet her impossibly high standards. The resulting pattern is a vicious cycle where cognitive distortions feed into obsessive doubt, further reinforcing the grip of OCD.

Strategies to Overcome Perfectionism

Cognitive-Behavioral Techniques

Cognitive-behavioral therapy (CBT) offers effective strategies for breaking the cycle of perfectionism in OCD. One core component of CBT is identifying and challenging irrational thoughts. By learning to recognize cognitive distortions—such as all-or-nothing thinking—women can begin to dismantle the unrealistic standards that drive their obsessive behaviors.

One practical CBT exercise involves writing down the perfectionistic thought, examining the evidence for and against it, and then re-framing it into a more balanced perspective. For example, rather than thinking, "If I don't get every detail right, I'm a failure," a more realistic thought might be, "Mistakes are a part of being human, and I can learn from them without diminishing my worth." Over time, these cognitive shifts can help weaken the power of perfectionism over one's self-esteem and behavior.

Exposure and Response Prevention (ERP)

Another valuable technique is Exposure and Response Prevention (ERP), which is especially useful in treating OCD. ERP involves deliberately confronting the fear of imperfection and resisting the urge to perform compulsive behaviors. For women with perfectionism-driven OCD, ERP might include deliberately leaving a task unfinished or accepting a minor mistake without engaging in ritualistic checking or correction.

While ERP can be challenging, it provides a powerful opportunity to experience that the feared consequences of imperfection are often far less devastating than imagined. Over repeated exposures, the anxiety associated with imperfection gradually decreases, paving the way for a more balanced and compassionate approach to self-evaluation.

Cultivating Self-Compassion

A critical antidote to perfectionism is self-compassion—the practice of treating oneself with the kindness and understanding that one would offer to a good friend. Women with OCD are often their harshest critics, and learning to replace self-judgment with self-compassion is a transformative step in recovery.

Self-compassion involves recognizing that mistakes are part of the human experience and that imperfection does not diminish one's inherent worth. Techniques such as mindful self-compassion exercises, journaling, and guided meditations can help women develop a more nurturing internal dialogue. Over time, this shift in perspective can alleviate the pressure to be perfect and reduce the intensity of obsessive thoughts.

Practical Exercises for Daily Life

Integrating these strategies into daily life is essential for long-term change. Here are a few practical exercises to consider:

- **Mindful Awareness:** Set aside a few minutes each day to practice mindfulness. Focus on your breath, notice any perfectionistic thoughts as they arise, and gently guide your attention back to the present moment.
- **Gratitude Journaling:** Maintain a daily journal where you write down three things you accomplished or appreciated about yourself, regardless of how "imperfect" the day may have been.
- **Setting Realistic Goals:** Break larger tasks into smaller, manageable steps with achievable outcomes. Celebrate small wins rather than waiting for a flawless result.
- **Affirmation Practice:** Develop a series of affirmations that counteract perfectionistic thoughts. Phrases like "I am enough," "Mistakes are opportunities to learn," or "Perfection is not a measure of my worth" can serve as powerful reminders during challenging moments.

Real-Life Stories of Transformation

To illustrate the impact of perfectionism on OCD and the transformative power of these strategies, consider the story of Sarah, a marketing executive who had long struggled with the relentless need to be perfect at work. Sarah's days were dominated by the fear of making even a minor error, which led her to double-check every report and obsess over every presentation. The stress of maintaining this façade not only impacted her professional performance but also strained her personal relationships.

After seeking help through therapy, Sarah began to identify the perfectionistic beliefs that were at the root of her anxiety. With the guidance of her therapist, she gradually implemented CBT techniques and ERP exercises. She learned to challenge the all-or-nothing thinking that had defined her approach to work. Over time, Sarah discovered that small mistakes did not spell disaster; rather, they were opportunities to learn and grow. By embracing imperfection and cultivating self-compassion, she was able to reduce the compulsive behaviors that had once controlled her life.

Similarly, Maria—a new mother with postpartum OCD—experienced overwhelming pressure to be the "perfect" parent. Every decision about her baby was fraught with doubt, and even the slightest deviation from her ideal of motherhood triggered intense anxiety and obsessive rituals. Through a combination of CBT, self-compassion exercises, and support from other mothers in a similar situation, Maria learned that imperfection was not a reflection of her love or capability. Instead, she began to view her journey as a series of learning experiences. The gradual acceptance of imperfection allowed her to experience motherhood with more ease and joy, rather than constant self-scrutiny.

Embracing Imperfection as a Path to Freedom

The journey to overcoming perfectionism in the context of OCD is not about lowering standards or settling for mediocrity. Rather, it is about recognizing that the relentless pursuit of perfection can be counterproductive and emotionally draining. Embracing imperfection means acknowledging that flaws and mistakes are an inevitable part of life—and that they can even serve as catalysts for growth, creativity, and deeper self-understanding.

When women learn to let go of the impossible standard of perfection, they open the door to a more authentic way of living. This shift not only alleviates the burden of obsessive thoughts but also fosters a greater sense of freedom and self-acceptance. In this new space, the focus shifts from constantly monitoring and correcting every detail to embracing life with all its inherent unpredictability and beauty.

Moving Forward

As we close this chapter, it is important to remember that the battle against perfectionism is ongoing. There will be days when old patterns resurface, when the voice of the inner critic becomes louder, and when the pressure to be perfect feels overwhelming. However, armed with the strategies discussed in this chapter—cognitive-behavioral techniques, exposure and response prevention, and a commitment to self-compassion—each setback can be viewed as an opportunity to practice and strengthen new, healthier ways of thinking.

The path to recovery is rarely linear. It is a winding journey filled with moments of doubt, breakthroughs, and continuous learning. Yet, with every step taken toward embracing imperfection, women with OCD can reclaim a sense of control and foster a more compassionate relationship with themselves.

This chapter has aimed to shed light on the intricate relationship between perfectionism and OCD in women. By understanding how societal pressures, early experiences, and cognitive distortions converge to create a high-stakes environment of self-criticism, readers can begin to untangle the web of expectations that has long governed their lives. More importantly, the chapter has provided practical tools and real-life examples to inspire hope and resilience in the face of perfectionism.

As you move forward, remember that each day offers a fresh opportunity to challenge the notion that perfection is the only acceptable standard. In learning to embrace the beauty of imperfection, you are not only diminishing the power of OCD but also creating space for authentic growth, self-compassion, and lasting change.

Welcome to the next phase of your journey—a phase where the quest for perfection gives way to a celebration of your humanity, where every misstep is seen as a stepping stone toward a fuller, more empowered life.

4

Unraveling "Pure O" and Intrusive Thoughts

Obsessive-compulsive disorder is often stereotyped by its visible rituals—excessive cleaning, checking, or ordering. However, many women experience a variant known as "Pure O," where the compulsions manifest not in observable behaviors, but in the form of intrusive thoughts and mental rituals. This chapter examines the intricate nature of "Pure O," delves into the psychology behind intrusive thoughts, and offers insights through case studies and references to seminal works in the field.

Understanding "Pure O"

"Pure O" is a term used to describe a type of OCD where the primary symptoms are obsessive thoughts without the accompanying overt compulsions. Despite its name, "Pure O" is not devoid of rituals; rather, the rituals occur internally. Individuals experiencing this form of OCD may engage in covert mental acts—such as silently repeating phrases, mentally reviewing scenarios, or compulsively analyzing thoughts—to neutralize the anxiety that arises from their intrusive thoughts.

In her groundbreaking work, *Overcoming Unwanted Intrusive Thoughts*,

Sally Winston explains that these internal compulsions can be just as debilitating as physical rituals. Women experiencing "Pure O" often struggle with a sense of isolation because their symptoms are not as outwardly visible, which can lead to misunderstandings by friends, family, and even mental health professionals.

The Nature of Intrusive Thoughts

Intrusive thoughts in "Pure O" can be startling, distressing, and entirely contrary to an individual's values. These thoughts might involve themes of harm, taboo sexual content, blasphemy, or even self-doubt about one's moral integrity. Importantly, these thoughts are unwanted and typically provoke intense guilt and anxiety. The paradox is that the very presence of these distressing thoughts often leads the individual to question their own character, even though the thoughts themselves are a symptom of OCD, not a reflection of personal desire or morality.

For example, a woman might experience intrusive thoughts about accidentally harming someone she loves, or she might have persistent doubts about having done something terribly wrong even when no mistake has occurred. The distress from these thoughts is not rooted in any real intent but in the irrational interpretations fueled by OCD. This phenomenon is well documented in Jonathan Grayson's book, *Freedom from Obsessive Compulsive Disorder*, where he emphasizes that understanding the nature of intrusive thoughts is a critical first step in reclaiming one's mental space.

Cognitive Processes Behind Intrusive Thoughts

Intrusive thoughts are sustained by cognitive distortions and a heightened state of anxiety. Women with "Pure O" may find themselves caught in a cycle of rumination where the brain fixates on one or two thoughts until they feel resolved—even though "resolution" is an illusion. This cycle is characterized by what cognitive-behavioral therapists refer to as "thought-action fusion," where the individual equates having an intrusive thought with actually carrying out the action. For instance, the mere thought of causing harm can be misinterpreted as evidence that harm will or could occur, even though these are irrational conclusions drawn from OCD.

A case study that illustrates this involves a woman named Rebecca, a 34-year-old teacher who began experiencing intrusive thoughts related to harming her students. Though Rebecca was deeply empathetic and devoted to her work, the irrational fear of being responsible for harm led her to engage in endless mental rituals—repeating the thought "I would never hurt anyone" over and over, scrutinizing every minor interaction for evidence of potential harm. With the support of a cognitive-behavioral therapist, Rebecca learned to challenge these thought distortions, gradually understanding that intrusive thoughts do not equate to intent or action. Her journey echoes the insights found in Jeffrey Schwartz's *Brain Lock*, where he outlines how recognizing the irrational nature of these thoughts is vital for recovery.

Mental Rituals: The Invisible Compulsions

Unlike physical compulsions, mental rituals are invisible to the outside observer, which can often leave women feeling misunderstood or even invalidated. These rituals might include counting, silently reciting specific phrases, or mentally reviewing every detail of an event. While these actions can temporarily reduce anxiety, they reinforce the obsessive cycle and perpetuate the belief that the only way to prevent harm is to engage in ritualistic thinking.

Consider the case of Laura, a 29-year-old graphic designer who battled with intrusive thoughts of contamination despite rarely encountering actual risks. Her mind would spiral into an endless loop of self-questioning and internal checking. Every time she entered a room or touched an object, she would mentally recite a sequence of words to "confirm" that she was safe. This behavior not only consumed hours of her day but also prevented her from engaging fully in her creative work and personal relationships. Laura's story, reminiscent of the personal accounts in *Overcoming Unwanted Intrusive Thoughts*, highlights how these internal rituals can be as disruptive as any overt compulsion.

The Emotional Toll of "Pure O"

The emotional impact of "Pure O" can be profound. The constant battle against intrusive thoughts often leads to feelings of shame, self-doubt, and isolation. Women may begin to internalize the notion that having such thoughts is a moral failing, leading to lowered self-esteem and a diminished sense of self-worth. The internal conflict—where one's deeply held values clash with the content of the intrusive thoughts—can be both confusing and deeply distressing.

A poignant case study is that of Maria, a new mother who began experiencing intrusive thoughts of harming her infant. The horror of these thoughts was compounded by the societal expectation that mothers are inherently nurturing and protective. Maria's internal struggle was so intense that she initially hesitated to seek help, fearing that her thoughts would define her as a bad parent. It was only after joining a support group and hearing similar stories that she realized her intrusive thoughts were a symptom of OCD and not a reflection of her true self. Maria's journey illustrates how understanding the irrational nature of intrusive thoughts, as discussed in *Freedom from Obsessive Compulsive Disorder*, can be transformative in reducing the associated guilt and anxiety.

Strategies for Managing Intrusive Thoughts

Cognitive-Behavioral Techniques

Cognitive-behavioral therapy (CBT) remains one of the most effective treatments for managing intrusive thoughts. One of the core strategies is to help individuals recognize and challenge the cognitive distortions that underpin their obsessions. For instance, a CBT exercise might involve writing down the intrusive thought, examining the evidence that supports and contradicts it, and then reframing it in a more rational, less threatening manner.

Rebecca, mentioned earlier, was taught to use a "thought diary" to document her intrusive thoughts and the subsequent mental rituals. Over time, by reviewing her diary with her therapist, she was able to identify patterns and challenge the automatic negative interpretations of her thoughts. This method is similar to techniques described in *Brain Lock*, where the emphasis is placed on interrupting the cycle of obsessive thinking through mindful awareness and cognitive restructuring.

Exposure and Response Prevention (ERP)

Exposure and Response Prevention (ERP) is another cornerstone of effective treatment for "Pure O." ERP involves intentionally exposing oneself to the thoughts that trigger anxiety, without engaging in the mental rituals that normally follow. Although ERP can be challenging—especially when the intrusive thoughts are deeply distressing—the gradual reduction in anxiety over time reinforces the understanding that the feared outcomes are unlikely to occur.

Laura, the graphic designer, participated in an ERP program where she deliberately allowed her intrusive thoughts to surface without resorting to her internal checking rituals. Initially, the anxiety was overwhelming, but with consistent practice and professional guidance, she began to notice a decrease in the intensity and frequency of her thoughts. ERP, as described in numerous clinical studies and referenced in works like *Overcoming Unwanted Intrusive Thoughts*, can be a powerful tool in dismantling the obsessive cycle.

Mindfulness and Acceptance

In recent years, mindfulness-based approaches have gained prominence as complementary techniques for managing intrusive thoughts. Mindfulness encourages individuals to observe their thoughts without judgment, creating a mental space where intrusive thoughts can arise and pass without triggering an emotional cascade. Acceptance and Commitment Therapy (ACT) builds on these principles, emphasizing that the goal is not to eliminate thoughts but to change one's relationship with them.

A case in point is a woman named Anita, who integrated mindfulness meditation into her daily routine. By practicing mindfulness, Anita learned to acknowledge her intrusive thoughts without immediately engaging in mental rituals. This shift in perspective allowed her to experience the thoughts as transient events rather than definitive statements of her character. Such mindfulness practices are highlighted in contemporary literature on OCD, providing an alternative pathway for those who may not respond fully to traditional CBT alone.

Integrating Case Studies and Lessons from Other Works

The experiences of women like Rebecca, Laura, and Maria illustrate that "Pure O" is not a monolithic condition; it manifests in various forms and intensities. Each case reinforces the notion that while intrusive thoughts are common, the way they are processed and managed can vary widely.

This variability is why tailored treatment plans are essential.

Several other influential books have contributed to the broader understanding of "Pure O" and intrusive thoughts. For instance, *The Imp of the Mind* by Lee Baer delves into the concept of intrusive thoughts from a neuropsychological perspective, emphasizing that these thoughts are not inherently dangerous but become problematic through the patterns of response they provoke. Similarly, *When in Doubt, Do Nothing* by Reid Wilson offers practical advice on resisting the urge to engage in compulsive rituals, reinforcing the importance of trust—in oneself and in the therapeutic process.

These works, along with the case studies presented in this chapter, serve as both educational tools and sources of hope for women grappling with "Pure O." They highlight that recovery is not about eradicating intrusive thoughts completely but about changing the way these thoughts are managed and perceived.

Moving Toward Empowerment

A key element in overcoming "Pure O" is empowerment—learning that intrusive thoughts do not have to define one's identity. The process involves cultivating self-compassion, understanding that these thoughts are a symptom of a treatable disorder, and developing practical strategies to manage them. It is vital for women to recognize that the distress they experience is not a personal failing but a reflection of a condition that can be addressed with appropriate support and intervention.

Support groups and therapy communities can play an instrumental role in this journey. Sharing experiences and learning from others who have faced similar challenges not only validates one's own experience but also fosters a sense of community and resilience. Many women find solace in knowing that they are not alone, and that recovery is a collaborative process.

Conclusion

Unraveling "Pure O" and its accompanying intrusive thoughts is a complex but essential part of understanding OCD in women. The invisible nature of these symptoms often leads to a heightened sense of isolation and self-doubt. However, as the case studies of Rebecca, Laura, Maria, and Anita illustrate, with the right combination of cognitive-behavioral techniques, ERP, mindfulness practices, and professional support, it is possible to reclaim one's mental space and break free from the grip of OCD.

By referencing established works like *Brain Lock*, *Freedom from Obsessive Compulsive Disorder*, and *Overcoming Unwanted Intrusive Thoughts*, we can see that the field of OCD treatment is both rich and evolving. These texts offer valuable insights and practical strategies that have helped countless women manage their intrusive thoughts and internal rituals. The collective wisdom of these resources, along with personalized case studies, provides a roadmap toward a future where intrusive thoughts no longer dictate one's self-worth or daily functioning.

In embracing the challenge of "Pure O," women are invited to see their intrusive thoughts not as harbingers of inevitable harm or moral failing, but as signals that change is needed—a call to engage in practices that promote mental resilience and self-acceptance. Each step taken in understanding and addressing these thoughts is a victory over the patterns that have long held them captive.

As you move forward from this chapter, remember that recovery is not about perfection or the complete eradication of intrusive thoughts. It is about building a new relationship with your mind—one characterized by compassion, understanding, and empowerment. In doing so, you not only alleviate the burden of "Pure O" but also open the door to a richer, more authentic experience of life.

Welcome to the journey of transformation, where every intrusive thought becomes an opportunity to grow, and every moment of clarity brings you closer to the freedom you deserve.

5

Beyond Rituals – The Emotional Cost of OCD

Obsessive-compulsive disorder is often discussed in terms of its overt rituals or hidden compulsions. However, one of the most profound—and sometimes overlooked—elements of OCD is the emotional toll it exacts. In this chapter, we delve into the often-invisible emotional costs that women pay when living with OCD. By examining the interplay between obsessive thoughts, compulsive behaviors, and deep-seated feelings of shame and isolation, we can better understand the true impact of the disorder on emotional well-being. We will also reference seminal works in the field and share case studies that illustrate these struggles in real life.

The Weight of Invisible Battles

For many women, the daily experience of OCD is not just marked by intrusive thoughts or repetitive rituals—it is also defined by the heavy burden of emotional distress. This distress often stems from the constant inner critic that judges every thought and action as inadequate. Even in the absence of physical rituals, the unending cycle of self-doubt and internal turmoil can lead to profound feelings of anxiety, depression, and a diminished sense of self-worth.

In his classic book *Brain Lock*, Jeffrey Schwartz explains that OCD is as much an emotional struggle as it is a cognitive one. The constant barrage of obsessive thoughts triggers a cascade of negative emotions that can overwhelm an individual's capacity to cope. For many women, the pressure to conform to societal standards of perfection and nurturing amplifies these feelings, turning each day into a battle against not only intrusive thoughts but also the emotional scars they leave behind.

Emotional Isolation and Self-Stigma

One of the most challenging aspects of OCD is the sense of isolation it can foster. Because many of the disorder's symptoms are internal and invisible, women often feel misunderstood by those around them. This misunderstanding can lead to self-stigma—a harmful internalization of the negative judgments and misconceptions about mental illness. Women with OCD may feel that their struggles are a personal failing, a belief reinforced by both external societal pressures and the relentless self-criticism that the disorder engenders.

Consider the case of Emily, a 38-year-old social worker whose life appeared successful on the surface. Despite her professional achievements and caring nature, Emily battled constant feelings of worthlessness driven by OCD. Her intrusive thoughts and the resulting internal rituals left her feeling isolated, as if she were trapped in a mental prison that no one could see. Emily's story echoes the sentiments expressed in *The OCD Workbook*, which emphasizes that acknowledging the emotional cost of OCD is a crucial step toward recovery. Through therapy and peer support groups, Emily eventually learned to challenge the self-stigma that had clouded her self-perception, though the journey was long and fraught with setbacks.

The Double-Edged Sword of Perfectionism

Perfectionism is often at the heart of OCD, particularly among women who have been socialized to believe that their value is contingent upon flawless performance. The relentless pursuit of perfection can lead to a state of perpetual dissatisfaction, where even small mistakes are seen as catastrophic. This mindset not only fuels the obsessive-compulsive cycle but also exacts a significant emotional toll.

In her influential work *When Perfect Isn't Good Enough*, psychologist Brené Brown discusses how the drive for perfection can lead to feelings of inadequacy and chronic stress. For many women with OCD, every minor imperfection becomes a glaring reminder of their perceived failure, leading to intense feelings of guilt, shame, and anxiety. This internal pressure can erode self-esteem over time, making it difficult for individuals to celebrate their successes or even acknowledge their strengths.

A case study that illustrates this dynamic is that of Rachel, a high-achieving executive who was haunted by the fear of making mistakes. Despite her accolades and professional success, Rachel's life was dominated by an inner narrative that relentlessly criticized her for any perceived shortcoming. Every mistake—whether real or imagined—was magnified into a catastrophic event, leaving her emotionally drained and constantly on edge. Through cognitive-behavioral therapy (CBT) and guided exercises that challenged her perfectionistic beliefs, Rachel gradually learned to reframe her thinking. However, the process was slow, underscoring the deep emotional roots of perfectionism in OCD.

The Role of Guilt and Self-Blame

Guilt is a common companion to OCD. Many women with the disorder experience a pervasive sense of guilt that stems from their intrusive thoughts, particularly when those thoughts involve themes that clash with their deeply held values. This guilt is often irrational—stemming not from any deliberate wrongdoing, but from the disorder's misinterpretation of harmless thoughts as evidence of moral failing.

For example, a mother might be tormented by intrusive thoughts about unintentionally harming her child. Even though these thoughts are entirely unwanted and recognized as irrational, the emotional impact is devastating. The guilt and self-blame can be so overwhelming that they lead to severe anxiety and even depressive episodes. Maria, a new mother featured in several clinical studies, shared how her intrusive thoughts made her feel unworthy of being a parent. It wasn't until she began working with a therapist, using techniques outlined in *Freedom from Obsessive Compulsive Disorder*, that she was able to understand that these thoughts were symptoms of OCD—not reflections of her character or abilities as a mother.

Depression, Anxiety, and the Cumulative Toll

It is not uncommon for women with OCD to experience comorbid conditions such as depression and generalized anxiety disorder. The cumulative toll of battling OCD—combined with the pressures of daily life—can lead to a state of chronic emotional exhaustion. The interplay between anxiety and depression creates a vicious cycle: obsessive thoughts lead to anxiety, which in turn fuels depressive feelings, further impairing one's ability to manage the disorder effectively.

In *The Mindfulness Solution for Anxiety*, author Ronald Siegel emphasizes that mindfulness practices can help break this cycle by promoting acceptance and emotional balance. By incorporating mindfulness into their daily routines, many women with OCD have found relief from the relentless emotional pressure that characterizes the disorder. This approach is echoed in the experiences of many clients, one of whom, Laura, a freelance writer, found that a daily mindfulness meditation routine reduced her anxiety levels and helped her manage the depressive moods that had long accompanied her OCD.

The Impact on Relationships and Social Life

OCD's emotional toll extends beyond the individual—it often affects relationships and social interactions as well. The constant inner battle can make it difficult for women to engage fully with others, leading to feelings of isolation and loneliness. The need to hide one's struggles, combined with the fear of being misunderstood or judged, can create barriers to intimacy and genuine connection.

For instance, consider the story of Anna, a 45-year-old teacher who gradually withdrew from social events due to the anxiety and shame associated with her OCD symptoms. Her reluctance to share her experiences with close friends and family led to misunderstandings and a growing sense of isolation. Anna's experience is not unique; many women report that the stigma surrounding mental health—and particularly OCD—forces them to retreat from supportive relationships. Works like *The Noonday Demon* by Andrew Solomon highlight the pervasive nature of mental health stigma and its impact on social interactions. Anna's journey toward recovery involved not only managing her OCD symptoms but also learning to communicate openly with her loved ones, thereby rebuilding her social support network.

Strategies to Mitigate Emotional Distress

Cognitive-Behavioral Therapy (CBT) for Emotional Resilience

CBT is a cornerstone of effective OCD treatment, and its benefits extend beyond the reduction of ritualistic behaviors. Through CBT, women learn to identify and challenge the irrational thoughts that underlie their emotional distress. Techniques such as thought restructuring and behavioral experiments can help dismantle the negative self-talk that fuels feelings of guilt and inadequacy.

A practical exercise often recommended in CBT involves keeping a daily journal of intrusive thoughts and the emotions they trigger. Over time, this practice helps in recognizing patterns and developing strategies to counteract them. For example, transforming a thought like "I am a terrible mother" into "I am doing my best and learning every day" can gradually shift the emotional response from guilt to empowerment. This method is supported by numerous case studies and clinical experiences detailed in *The OCD Workbook*, which many therapists use as a guide in treatment sessions.

Mindfulness and Acceptance-Based Approaches

Mindfulness and acceptance-based therapies have shown considerable promise in mitigating the emotional distress associated with OCD. By learning to observe their thoughts without judgment, women can develop a healthier relationship with the intrusive ideas that once seemed overwhelming. This practice allows for a shift in focus—from trying to eliminate negative thoughts to accepting them as transient mental events that do not define one's self-worth.

One powerful example is found in the work of Anita, a woman who integrated mindfulness practices into her recovery plan. Initially overwhelmed by the emotional fallout of her intrusive thoughts, Anita began practicing daily mindfulness meditation. Over several months, she noticed a marked reduction in her anxiety and an improved ability to manage depressive moods. Her story is reminiscent of the techniques described in *The Mindfulness Solution for Anxiety*, demonstrating that with patience and practice, mindfulness can serve as a potent antidote to the emotional turbulence of OCD.

Building a Support Network

No discussion of emotional well-being is complete without acknowledging the importance of a robust support network. Peer support groups, family therapy, and even online communities can provide a much-needed sense of belonging and validation. Sharing experiences with others who understand the unique challenges of OCD can alleviate the burden of isolation and help women realize that they are not alone in their struggles.

Take, for example, the case of Sarah, a 32-year-old graphic designer who felt isolated by her OCD. When Sarah joined a local support group for women with OCD, she discovered a community where her experiences were understood and validated. The connections she made not only provided emotional relief but also reinforced the message that recovery is possible when one has a supportive network. Such stories echo the sentiments in *When Perfect Isn't Good Enough*, which emphasizes the transformative power of shared experiences and community support.

Looking to the Future: Embracing Emotional Healing

The emotional cost of OCD is significant, but it is not insurmountable. As we continue to explore the multifaceted nature of this disorder, it is important to remember that healing involves both managing symptoms and addressing the deeper emotional wounds they cause. Recovery is a gradual process—one that requires self-compassion, patience, and the willingness to seek help when needed.

The literature on OCD consistently highlights that emotional healing is a critical component of overall recovery. By addressing not only the behaviors but also the underlying feelings of guilt, shame, and isolation, women can pave the way for more sustainable, long-term improvement. Seminal works such as *Brain Lock* and *Freedom from Obsessive Compulsive Disorder* remind us that while the journey is challenging, each step toward emotional resilience is a victory.

Conclusion

In this chapter, we have explored the profound emotional cost of OCD—a cost that extends far beyond the visible rituals or mental compulsions. We have seen how intrusive thoughts, perfectionistic pressures, and the relentless inner critic can lead to feelings of isolation, depression, and anxiety. Through case studies of individuals like Emily, Rachel, Maria, Anna, and Sarah, we have gained insight into the diverse ways in which OCD impacts emotional well-being.

By integrating therapeutic strategies such as cognitive-behavioral therapy, mindfulness, and building supportive communities, women can begin to dismantle the emotional barriers that have long held them back. The journey to emotional healing is not linear, and setbacks are part of the process. However, every effort made to challenge negative thought patterns and build self-compassion brings one closer to a life defined not by the weight of OCD, but by the resilience and strength of the individual.

As you continue on this journey of recovery, remember that the emotional wounds inflicted by OCD do not have to be permanent. With the right tools, professional guidance, and a supportive network, healing is possible. Embrace each moment of progress, no matter how small, and recognize that every step forward is a testament to your courage and determination.

The path to recovery is a long one, but it is also a path toward a richer, more authentic life—one where the emotional cost of OCD no longer defines you. Welcome to a future where you can reclaim your emotional well-being and move forward with hope, resilience, and a deep sense of self-worth.

6

The Hidden Battle – OCD and Motherhood

Motherhood is often portrayed as a time of joy, bonding, and fulfillment. Yet, for many women with OCD, this period is also marked by an intense internal struggle—a hidden battle that often remains unspoken. In this chapter, we explore how OCD manifests during motherhood, especially in the postpartum period, and how maternal OCD can differ from other forms of the disorder. By examining both clinical insights and personal case studies, and referencing established works in the field, we aim to shed light on the unique challenges faced by mothers who wrestle with intrusive thoughts and obsessive doubts.

The Complexity of Maternal OCD

Obsessive-compulsive disorder, in the context of motherhood, can present with distinctive features. Unlike more commonly recognized forms of OCD that may involve repetitive cleaning or checking behaviors, maternal OCD often involves intrusive thoughts related to the safety and well-being of one's child. These thoughts are typically distressing, unwanted, and contrary to the nurturing instincts of a mother. They can include fears of harming the baby, doubts about being a good parent, or irrational worries about potential dangers—from leaving the house with the baby to even fears about the baby's health arising from mundane situations.

In *Freedom from Obsessive Compulsive Disorder*, Jonathan Grayson explains that OCD thrives on uncertainty. For mothers, the overwhelming sense of responsibility for another human being magnifies this uncertainty, making intrusive thoughts not only more frequent but also more emotionally charged. The stakes seem impossibly high; every decision, every moment alone with the baby, is subject to obsessive scrutiny.

Postpartum OCD: When Joy Meets Anxiety

The postpartum period is a time of significant hormonal, emotional, and lifestyle changes. While many new mothers experience a range of emotions—from elation to exhaustion—some also face the onset or worsening of OCD symptoms. Postpartum OCD is characterized by intrusive thoughts and compulsions that revolve around the baby's well-being. These might include repetitive checking to ensure the baby is breathing, constant mental reviews of caregiving routines, or even distressing images and fears that challenge a mother's self-image as protective and loving.

In her influential book *The Mommy Myth*, Susan Douglas discusses how societal expectations of the "perfect mother" can intensify the pressure new mothers feel. This societal ideal often leaves little room for the natural anxieties of parenthood. When a mother experiences intrusive thoughts—such as sudden images of harm coming to her child—the internal narrative can spiral into self-blame and overwhelming guilt. These thoughts, though recognized as irrational by the mother herself, feel deeply real and can lead to compulsive behaviors aimed at "neutralizing" the danger, even when no external threat exists.

The Psychological Underpinnings of Maternal OCD

Understanding maternal OCD requires delving into its psychological roots. Several factors contribute to the emergence of OCD during motherhood:

1. **Heightened Responsibility and Fear of Harm:** The transition to motherhood brings with it an immense responsibility. The intense focus on the baby's safety can activate an overactive threat-detection system in the brain. This heightened sensitivity, combined with a natural parental instinct to protect, can cause intrusive thoughts to flourish.
2. **Perfectionism and the Ideal Mother:** As discussed in Chapter 3, perfectionism is a key component in many women's OCD experiences. The pressure to be the "perfect mother" exacerbates self-doubt and fosters an environment in which any deviation from the ideal is met with harsh self-criticism. In this context, even fleeting intrusive thoughts can trigger profound anxiety.
3. **Hormonal Fluctuations:** Biological changes during and after pregnancy are significant. Fluctuating hormone levels can affect neurotransmitter systems in the brain, which may, in turn, intensify OCD symptoms. Research has suggested that postpartum hormonal shifts can exacerbate existing anxiety disorders, including OCD.
4. **Sleep Deprivation and Stress:** New motherhood often comes with chronic sleep deprivation and heightened stress. These factors can lower the threshold for anxiety and make it more challenging for the brain to regulate intrusive thoughts. The constant state of alertness required to care for a newborn can leave little room for the mental rest that is crucial for managing OCD.

Real-Life Case Studies: Mothers in the Midst of the Battle

Case Study 1: *Maria's Journey Through Postpartum Intrusions*

Maria, a 31-year-old first-time mother, experienced the full force of postpartum OCD shortly after the birth of her daughter. Maria's intrusive thoughts were centered on fears that she might accidentally harm her baby while trying to care for her. These thoughts would come unbidden in the middle of the night, during quiet moments of feeding, or even when simply looking away for a split second. Despite her deep love for her child, these images and ideas filled her with dread and self-reproach.

After several months of isolation and mounting anxiety, Maria sought help from a therapist who specialized in perinatal mental health. Through a combination of cognitive-behavioral therapy (CBT) and exposure and response prevention (ERP), Maria began to dismantle the cycle of fear. Her therapist introduced her to the concept of "thought-action fusion"—the mistaken belief that having a thought is equivalent to carrying out the action—and helped her challenge this misconception. By learning to observe her thoughts without judgment and resist the urge to engage in compulsive checking (such as repeatedly confirming that her baby was safe), Maria gradually reclaimed control over her mind. Her progress is reminiscent of strategies discussed in *Freedom from Obsessive Compulsive Disorder*, which emphasize that recovery is a gradual process that involves reshaping one's relationship with intrusive thoughts.

Case Study 2: *Laura's Battle with Maternal Doubt*

Laura, a 28-year-old mother of two, experienced a different facet of maternal OCD. For her, the obsessions were less about direct harm and more about doubts regarding her capabilities as a parent. She was plagued by the belief that she was not nurturing enough, that every decision she made might inadvertently compromise her children's well-being. These thoughts led to compulsive behaviors such as endless research, over-preparation for everyday tasks, and seeking constant reassurance from family members and pediatricians.

Laura's turning point came when she attended a support group for mothers dealing with postpartum anxiety and OCD. Hearing the stories of other women who faced similar challenges helped her understand that her intrusive thoughts were not a personal failing but a common manifestation of OCD. Through group therapy and individual counseling, Laura learned to reframe her thoughts. Techniques borrowed from mindfulness-based cognitive therapy (MBCT) allowed her to develop a kinder internal dialogue and reduce her self-criticism. Her experience, which mirrors insights found in *The Mommy Myth* and other works on maternal mental health, underscores the importance of community and shared understanding in overcoming the isolation that often accompanies maternal OCD.

Navigating the Dual Identity: Mother and Warrior Against OCD

The journey of a mother battling OCD is one of navigating dual identities—one of nurturer and caregiver, and the other of a person grappling with intrusive fears and compulsions. This duality can create an internal conflict, as mothers often feel torn between the need to protect their children and the need to care for their own mental health.

In the words of Brené Brown in *Daring Greatly*, vulnerability is not a sign of weakness but of courage. For mothers with OCD, embracing vulnerability means acknowledging the existence of intrusive thoughts and seeking help without shame. It involves recognizing that being an effective parent does not require perfection but rather the willingness to face and manage one's own struggles.

Treatment Modalities Tailored for Maternal OCD

Given the unique challenges posed by maternal OCD, treatment modalities often need to be adapted to address both the mental health of the mother and her role as a caregiver. Here are several approaches that have proven effective:

1. Specialized Cognitive-Behavioral Therapy (CBT)

CBT for maternal OCD typically focuses on identifying and challenging the irrational beliefs that underpin intrusive thoughts about the baby's safety or the mother's competence. Techniques such as thought records and cognitive restructuring are used to help mothers differentiate between irrational fears and realistic concerns. Therapists often work with mothers to develop strategies for gradual exposure to anxiety-provoking situations—like leaving the baby momentarily in a safe environment—while preventing the urge to perform compulsive behaviors.

2. Exposure and Response Prevention (ERP)

ERP is considered one of the most effective treatments for OCD. For mothers, ERP might involve controlled exposure to the situations that trigger intrusive thoughts, paired with strategies to resist the corresponding compulsions. For example, a mother who fears that a momentary lapse in attention will endanger her child might practice briefly delaying the urge to check on the baby repeatedly. Over time, ERP helps reduce the anxiety associated with these thoughts, reinforcing the understanding that the feared outcomes are unlikely.

3. Mindfulness and Acceptance Techniques

Mindfulness practices can empower mothers to observe their intrusive thoughts without immediate reaction. Acceptance and Commitment Therapy (ACT) encourages mothers to accept the presence of intrusive thoughts as temporary mental events rather than definitive truths. By focusing on the present moment and engaging in mindful breathing or meditation, mothers can develop a more balanced relationship with their anxiety. This approach is supported by literature such as *The Mindfulness Solution for Anxiety*, which outlines practical exercises to help individuals cultivate acceptance and reduce emotional reactivity.

4. Hormonal and Lifestyle Considerations

Given that hormonal fluctuations can exacerbate OCD symptoms, some treatment plans incorporate strategies to manage these biological changes. This might include regular sleep schedules, balanced nutrition, and, in some cases, medical interventions to stabilize hormonal levels. Addressing lifestyle factors is crucial, as chronic sleep deprivation and high stress can make it even more challenging to manage OCD symptoms effectively.

5. Support Networks and Peer Groups

Building a robust support network is essential for mothers with OCD. Joining support groups—whether in person or online—provides a safe space to share experiences and receive validation from others who understand the unique challenges of maternal OCD. The collective wisdom and empathy found in these communities can be a powerful antidote to isolation and self-stigma.

Integrating Lessons from the Literature

Several influential works have shed light on the interplay between motherhood and OCD. For example, in *When in Doubt, Do Nothing*, Reid Wilson emphasizes the importance of resisting the compulsion to overreact to intrusive thoughts—a lesson that resonates deeply with many mothers. Similarly, *Freedom from Obsessive Compulsive Disorder* provides detailed accounts of how intrusive thoughts can be managed through cognitive and behavioral strategies, offering hope and practical advice to those grappling with the disorder.

By integrating these lessons into therapy, many mothers have found that understanding the broader context of OCD can help demystify their experiences and reduce the sense of personal failure. Recognizing that intrusive thoughts are a symptom of a treatable disorder—and not a reflection of one's worth as a parent—can be transformative in the journey toward recovery.

Moving Forward: Embracing Imperfection in Motherhood

The path to recovery for mothers with OCD is not about achieving perfection; it is about learning to live with uncertainty while maintaining a nurturing relationship with oneself. Embracing imperfection means acknowledging that intrusive thoughts may never disappear entirely, but their impact can be diminished through effective coping strategies, self-compassion, and professional support.

It is vital for mothers to remember that seeking help is a sign of strength, not weakness. The dual challenge of caring for a child and managing OCD requires courage, and every step taken toward recovery is a victory. As Brené Brown reminds us, vulnerability and authenticity pave the way for connection and healing.

Maternal OCD is a hidden battle—a struggle that often unfolds in silence, beneath the surface of the joys and challenges of motherhood. In this chapter, we have explored the complex interplay between intrusive thoughts, maternal responsibilities, and the overwhelming pressure to be perfect. Through the real-life stories of mothers like Maria and Laura, and by referencing influential works such as *Freedom from Obsessive Compulsive Disorder* and *The Mommy Myth*, we have seen that maternal OCD is not a reflection of inadequate parenting but rather a manifestation of a treatable mental health condition.

By tailoring treatment modalities—ranging from specialized CBT and ERP to mindfulness practices and support groups—mothers can begin to reclaim their lives and redefine what it means to be a good parent. Recovery is a gradual process, filled with setbacks and triumphs alike, but each step forward is a testament to the resilience and strength of the human spirit.

As you move forward on your journey, remember that your value as a mother is not measured by the absence of intrusive thoughts, but by your willingness to seek help, to adapt, and to embrace the imperfections that make you uniquely human. The hidden battle of maternal OCD may be challenging, but it is also an opportunity to discover inner strength, foster deeper connections, and ultimately create a more authentic, fulfilling life for both you and your child.

Welcome to a future where the challenges of OCD are met with understanding, compassion, and effective strategies—a future where motherhood is celebrated not in spite of its imperfections, but because of them.

7

The Impact of Relationships and Social Expectations

OCD does not exist in a vacuum. For many women, its effects extend far beyond the individual mind—they ripple out into relationships, social interactions, and the expectations imposed by society. In this chapter, we will explore how OCD affects personal relationships, how social norms and expectations amplify its effects, and what steps can be taken to foster healthier interactions. Drawing on insights from seminal works like Brain Lock and The OCD Workbook, and weaving in real-life case studies, we aim to provide a comprehensive understanding of how social dynamics interact with OCD and offer practical strategies for overcoming these challenges.

The Intersection of OCD and Personal Relationships

OCD has a unique way of infiltrating close relationships. It may not always be immediately visible to outsiders, but for those who live with it, the disorder can create significant barriers to intimacy and trust. The internal struggle—characterized by intrusive thoughts and compulsive behaviors—often spills over into interactions with partners, family members, and friends.

The Strain on Romantic Partnerships

Romantic relationships require vulnerability and trust, yet for women with OCD, revealing the hidden battles inside their minds can feel daunting. Many fear that sharing their intrusive thoughts or compulsive behaviors will lead to judgment or rejection. This fear is compounded by societal narratives that idealize flawless, supportive relationships. In *The OCD Workbook*, Bruce Hyman and Cherry Pedrick explain that partners may inadvertently reinforce OCD behaviors by offering reassurance or becoming entangled in the rituals themselves. For instance, a husband might find himself repeatedly asked to validate that everything is "just right" before leaving the house, gradually feeling burdened by the responsibility.

A case study that illustrates this is that of Laura, a 35-year-old marketing professional who struggled with "pure O" intrusions that affected her relationship with her long-term partner, Mark. Laura's intrusive thoughts often centered around fears of harming her loved ones or failing as a partner. Instead of discussing these thoughts openly, she resorted to subtle rituals and secretive behaviors. Mark, initially puzzled by her sudden need for reassurance, eventually felt sidelined, unsure how to help without worsening her anxiety. Their relationship reached a critical point when both decided to attend couple's therapy. With guidance from a therapist well-versed in OCD dynamics, they learned strategies to communicate more openly. Mark was encouraged to provide steady support without becoming entangled in the rituals, while Laura learned to share her inner struggles without shame. This transformation echoes the lessons in *Brain Lock*, where Jeffrey Schwartz emphasizes that recovery is not just an individual journey but one that can be supported through empathetic and informed relationships.

Family Dynamics and the Weight of Expectations

Family relationships can be both a source of support and a significant stressor for women with OCD. Many women grow up in households where expectations are high, and the fear of disappointing loved ones is ever-present. These early experiences often lay the groundwork for the perfectionistic tendencies that later fuel OCD. In some cases, family members may unknowingly exacerbate the disorder by minimizing symptoms or by reinforcing the idea that any deviation from perfection is unacceptable.

Consider the case of Emily, a 28-year-old teacher whose family placed enormous emphasis on academic and personal achievement. From a young age, she was praised only for flawless performance. As an adult, Emily's OCD manifested in an endless cycle of self-doubt and compulsive checking, especially in professional and familial contexts. Her parents' inability to understand the emotional toll of her rituals led to misunderstandings and a sense of isolation within her own home. It was only when Emily sought help and her family attended educational sessions about OCD that a more supportive environment was fostered. Emily's experience, similar to many discussed in *The OCD Workbook*, underscores the importance of family education and the need to dismantle unrealistic expectations that can worsen OCD symptoms.

Friendships and Social Isolation

Social relationships outside the family and romantic partnerships also feel the impact of OCD. Women with the disorder may withdraw from social activities for fear of their intrusive thoughts being discovered or misunderstood. They might also avoid forming new friendships, fearing that others will judge them harshly for their "strange" behaviors. Over time, this isolation can lead to a vicious cycle: the more withdrawn a person becomes, the more intense their OCD symptoms can become, as there are fewer external supports to counterbalance internal criticisms.

A notable case involves Sarah, a 40-year-old freelance writer who became increasingly isolated as her OCD symptoms worsened. Sarah's intrusive thoughts were predominantly centered on fears of being a burden or failing to meet the expectations of her peers. Gradually, she stopped attending social gatherings and avoided reconnecting with old friends. It wasn't until she joined an online support group for women with OCD that Sarah began to rebuild her social network. Hearing others share similar experiences helped her realize that her struggles were not unique or shameful, but rather a common facet of living with OCD. This realization, which mirrors the insights found in Andrew Solomon's *The Noonday Demon*, was a turning point that enabled her to seek professional help and gradually re-engage with her social circle.

The Role of Social Expectations and Gender Norms

Beyond personal relationships, the broader social context plays a crucial role in shaping how women experience OCD. Social expectations—particularly those related to gender—can intensify the internal pressures that contribute to OCD. Women are often bombarded with messages about how they should look, behave, and succeed in multiple roles, such as being the perfect professional, partner, and mother. These multifaceted expectations create a fertile ground for OCD to flourish.

Societal Pressures and the Idealized Self

The pressure to maintain an idealized image is a common theme in the lives of many women with OCD. Advertisements, media portrayals, and even social media feeds reinforce the notion that perfection is not only desirable but necessary. In her book *When Perfect Isn't Good Enough*,

Brené Brown discusses how the relentless pursuit of perfection can lead to feelings of inadequacy and chronic anxiety. For women with OCD, this pressure becomes internalized, and every small deviation from the ideal is met with harsh self-judgment. The constant need to appear flawless can exacerbate the obsessive-compulsive cycle, as women strive to control every detail of their lives to conform to societal standards.

A case study highlighting these dynamics is that of Rebecca, a 33-year-old architect whose OCD was heavily influenced by societal expectations. Rebecca was known among her peers for her meticulous attention to detail and high standards at work. However, behind the veneer of competence lay an unrelenting fear of imperfection. Rebecca's intrusive thoughts often revolved around fears of public embarrassment and professional failure. Her attempts to control every aspect of her work and appearance left her exhausted and isolated. It wasn't until Rebecca began working with a therapist who specialized in treating perfectionism—a treatment approach discussed in *The Perfectionism Workbook* by Taylor Newendorp—that she learned to challenge these unrealistic expectations. Through therapy, she discovered that her worth was not tied to her ability to meet an impossible ideal, paving the way for healthier relationships both at work and at home.

The Impact of Cultural Narratives

Cultural narratives also play a significant role in shaping the experience of OCD. In many societies, traditional gender roles continue to dictate how women should behave—often placing an emphasis on selflessness, nurturance, and emotional labor. These roles can lead to an overwhelming sense of responsibility and self-sacrifice, which in turn feeds into obsessive thoughts and compulsions. Women may feel that they must always put others' needs before their own, even at the cost of their mental health.

For example, Anna, a 42-year-old mother of three, internalized the belief that her primary role was to care for her family, leaving little room for self-care. Anna's OCD manifested as an incessant need to ensure that every detail of her family's life was perfect—from meal planning to managing household schedules. The pressure to uphold these ideals led to significant anxiety and a feeling of being trapped in an endless cycle of obligations. Anna's experience reflects the insights found in *The Mommy Myth*, which critiques the unrealistic expectations placed on modern mothers. Through therapy and involvement in a community of like-minded women, Anna began to challenge the cultural narratives that had contributed to her stress, learning to set boundaries and prioritize her well-being without guilt.

Strategies for Navigating Relationships and Social Expectations

Building Open Communication Channels

One of the first steps toward mitigating the impact of OCD on relationships is fostering open and honest communication. Women with OCD are often reluctant to share the details of their struggles, fearing that their loved ones will not understand. However, research and clinical experience, as highlighted in *The OCD Stories* by Dean McKay, suggest that sharing personal experiences can lead to greater empathy and support.

For instance, couples therapy and family counseling can provide safe spaces for individuals to discuss how OCD affects their interactions. Practical exercises, such as role-playing or guided discussions, can help both the person with OCD and their loved ones understand the triggers and challenges associated with the disorder. This mutual understanding is essential in creating an environment where OCD is seen not as a personal failing but as a treatable condition.

Educating Loved Ones and Cultivating Empathy

Educating those in one's support network about OCD is a powerful way to reduce stigma and foster empathy. When friends, family, and partners understand that OCD is a neurobiological disorder rather than a choice or a character flaw, they are more likely to provide compassionate support. Several books, including *Brain Lock* and *Freedom from Obsessive Compulsive Disorder*, offer accessible explanations of the disorder that can be shared with loved ones. These resources help demystify OCD and promote an informed dialogue that benefits everyone involved.

Developing Assertive Self-Advocacy

Assertiveness is key for women with OCD, especially when navigating social expectations that feel overwhelming. Learning to advocate for one's own needs—whether in a work setting, in a relationship, or within the family—is an important step toward reducing the emotional burden of OCD. Assertive communication involves expressing one's feelings and setting boundaries without feeling guilty or fearing backlash. Workshops on assertiveness training and self-advocacy, often referenced in recovery literature, can empower women to reclaim their voices and make decisions that prioritize their mental health.

Engaging in Peer Support and Community Building

Connecting with others who understand the experience of OCD can be incredibly validating. Peer support groups—whether in person or online—offer a space where women can share their stories, exchange coping strategies, and build resilience. Many women find that knowing they are not alone in their struggles alleviates some of the isolation brought on by OCD. The communal wisdom gained through these interactions is invaluable, and it reinforces the idea that recovery is a collective process.

Looking Ahead: Cultivating a Balanced Social Life

Ultimately, the goal is not to eliminate OCD entirely but to learn to live with it in a way that minimizes its negative impact on relationships and social interactions. This involves cultivating a balanced social life where one's identity is not solely defined by the disorder. By challenging the unrealistic standards imposed by society and fostering more supportive and authentic relationships, women can begin to reclaim their sense of self.

Embracing vulnerability—as advocated by Brené Brown in Daring Greatly—can be transformative. Vulnerability in relationships allows for deeper connections and facilitates the kind of understanding that is essential for healing. When women are able to acknowledge their struggles openly, they not only pave the way for personal recovery but also help to dismantle the societal stigmas that have long surrounded OCD.

The impact of OCD on relationships and social expectations is profound and multifaceted. From the strain on romantic partnerships and family dynamics to the isolating effects of social stigma, OCD challenges women in ways that extend far beyond individual symptoms. However, by fostering open communication, educating loved ones, practicing assertive self-advocacy, and building supportive communities, women can begin to transform these challenges into opportunities for growth and connection.

Drawing on insights from key texts such as *Brain Lock*, *The OCD Workbook*, and *Daring Greatly*, as well as the real-life experiences of individuals like Laura, Emily, Rebecca, and Anna, it is clear that the journey toward healthier relationships is both possible and empowering. The strategies discussed in this chapter are not a cure-all; rather, they are tools that can help women navigate the complex interplay between OCD and social expectations.

As you move forward, remember that every step you take toward open communication and self-advocacy not only helps in managing OCD but also enriches your relationships and enhances your overall quality of life. Embrace the journey with patience, compassion, and the knowledge that you are not alone in this struggle.

Welcome to a future where your relationships are defined not by the limitations of OCD but by your resilience, authenticity, and the strength of your support network.

8

The Road to Recovery – Introduction to Cognitive-Behavioral Therapy (CBT)

The journey toward reclaiming control over OCD begins with understanding that recovery is possible—and that it starts with a practical, evidence-based approach to treatment. Cognitive-Behavioral Therapy (CBT) has long been established as one of the most effective interventions for managing and overcoming OCD symptoms. In this chapter, we introduce CBT as the cornerstone of recovery, explain its core principles, and illustrate its transformative potential through real-life case studies and references to seminal works in the field. This roadmap is designed to help you navigate the complexities of OCD and begin building a personalized recovery plan.

Understanding the Foundations of CBT

CBT is grounded in the idea that our thoughts, feelings, and behaviors are interconnected. For individuals with OCD, the disorder is maintained by maladaptive thought patterns—often irrational beliefs or cognitive distortions—that drive compulsive behaviors and exacerbate anxiety. CBT aims to break this cycle by helping you identify and challenge these unhelpful thoughts, and by teaching you strategies to modify your behavior in ways that reduce anxiety over time.

In his influential book *Brain Lock*, Jeffrey Schwartz outlines how OCD is not a moral failing but a condition rooted in the brain's circuitry. Schwartz explains that the brain can become "stuck" in a loop of obsessive thoughts and compulsive responses. CBT, especially its exposure and response prevention (ERP) component, helps "unlock" these patterns by gradually exposing you to anxiety-provoking situations without engaging in compulsive behaviors.

Key Components of CBT for OCD

- **Cognitive Restructuring:**
- Cognitive restructuring involves identifying the irrational or distorted thoughts that fuel OCD, evaluating their validity, and then reframing them into more balanced, rational perspectives. For example, a mother plagued by intrusive thoughts about harming her child might learn to reframe such thoughts as a symptom of her anxiety rather than an indication of her character.
- **Exposure and Response Prevention (ERP):**
- ERP is perhaps the most well-known element of CBT for OCD. It involves systematically confronting the situations or thoughts that trigger anxiety, without performing the ritualistic behaviors that normally serve to reduce that anxiety. Over time, repeated exposure helps diminish the power of these triggers, a process described in Reid Wilson's *When in Doubt, Do Nothing*, which emphasizes the importance of resisting compulsive responses.
- **Behavioral Experiments:**
- These are structured activities where you test out the reality behind your obsessive beliefs. By conducting behavioral experiments, you can gather evidence that contradicts your irrational fears, ultimately

reducing anxiety and boosting confidence in your ability to manage uncertainty.
- **Mindfulness and Acceptance:**
- While traditional CBT focuses on changing thought patterns, recent adaptations incorporate mindfulness techniques to help you observe your thoughts without judgment. This aspect of therapy is echoed in Ronald Siegel's *The Mindfulness Solution for Anxiety*, which advocates for a balanced approach where acceptance of transient thoughts is a stepping stone to recovery.

The Transformative Potential of CBT

The beauty of CBT lies in its structured approach and measurable progress. Recovery is not about eliminating OCD entirely—an impossible goal—but rather about reducing the intensity and frequency of intrusive thoughts and compulsions so that they no longer dominate your life. The shift from an environment of fear and avoidance to one of gradual confrontation and acceptance is a powerful transformation that many have experienced through CBT.

Case Study: Rebecca's Journey to Reclaim Control

Consider the case of Rebecca, a 34-year-old teacher who struggled with persistent intrusive thoughts related to harming her students—a fear that was completely out of character but nonetheless debilitating. Rebecca's symptoms were subtle; she did not exhibit overt compulsions but instead engaged in a series of mental rituals, such as repeatedly assuring herself that she would never act on her thoughts. These rituals provided only temporary relief and reinforced her anxiety.

Rebecca's therapist introduced her to CBT, starting with cognitive restructuring. Together, they identified the cognitive distortions that linked her intrusive thoughts to catastrophic outcomes. By maintaining a thought diary, Rebecca recorded her intrusive thoughts, the associated emotions, and the triggers. Over time, she began to see that her thoughts were not predictive of her actions. She then engaged in ERP, deliberately exposing herself to situations where her intrusive thoughts would occur—such as supervising her classroom—without performing her mental rituals. Gradually, Rebecca reported a decrease in her anxiety, and she learned to tolerate the discomfort of uncertainty. Her progress was a testament to the efficacy of CBT and is reminiscent of the strategies outlined in *Brain Lock*.

Case Study: Laura's Breakthrough with ERP

Laura, a graphic designer in her late twenties, experienced a variant of OCD characterized by "pure O"—obsessive thoughts with minimal visible compulsions. Her intrusive thoughts revolved around contamination fears, leading to constant internal rumination and mental checking rituals. Laura felt trapped in a cycle of self-doubt and anxiety, convinced that even a fleeting lapse in vigilance could lead to disaster.

Laura's treatment plan centered on ERP. With her therapist's guidance, she developed a hierarchy of feared situations, starting with scenarios that induced mild anxiety and gradually progressing to more challenging exposures. One exercise involved deliberately delaying her internal urge to mentally review every detail after touching objects in her workplace. At first, the anxiety was intense, but over several weeks of consistent practice, Laura noticed a significant reduction in both the frequency and intensity of her intrusive thoughts. Her journey, as documented in her therapy sessions, echoed the methods detailed in *When in Doubt, Do Nothing*—highlighting that recovery is achieved not by eliminating anxiety entirely but by learning to live with it without resorting to compulsions.

Integrating CBT into Daily Life

One of the key challenges of CBT is integrating its techniques into everyday routines. The goal is to make the skills learned in therapy a natural part of how you cope with stress and uncertainty. Here are some practical strategies to consider:

Developing a Structured Routine

Establishing a daily routine can provide a sense of predictability and control, which is particularly valuable for those with OCD. Incorporate time for:

- **Mindfulness Meditation:** A daily practice—even just 10 minutes—can help ground your thoughts and reduce the intensity of intrusive ideas.
- **Journaling:** Keeping a thought diary helps you track progress, recognize patterns, and reflect on the successes and setbacks along your journey.
- **Scheduled Exposures:** Identify moments in your day where you can deliberately confront triggers without resorting to compulsive behaviors. Over time, these exposures will build resilience.

Setting Realistic Goals

Recovery is not about achieving perfection—it's about incremental progress. Set small, achievable goals for each week. For example, if a particular situation causes significant anxiety, plan a controlled exposure and gradually increase the difficulty as your tolerance improves. Celebrate each victory, no matter how small, as a testament to your growing strength and resilience.

Seeking Professional Guidance

CBT is most effective when guided by a trained therapist who understands the nuances of OCD. A professional can help tailor the therapy to your specific needs, provide support during challenging exposures, and offer objective insights into your progress. If possible, consider joining a therapy group or online forum where you can share experiences and learn from others facing similar challenges.

The Role of Self-Compassion in CBT

An essential element of CBT is the development of self-compassion. For many women with OCD, the internal narrative is harsh and unforgiving. CBT teaches you to challenge this inner critic by replacing self-blame with self-acceptance. Techniques such as self-compassion meditation and affirmations help nurture a kinder internal dialogue.

Brené Brown's *Daring Greatly* provides an inspiring perspective on vulnerability and self-compassion. By embracing your imperfections, you create room for growth and healing. In therapy, you may be encouraged to practice self-compassion by writing a letter to yourself from the perspective of a supportive friend—acknowledging your struggles while also celebrating your courage to seek help.

The Importance of a Supportive Environment

Recovery is not an isolated process. Building a support network is crucial to sustaining the progress made through CBT. Share your journey with trusted friends, family, or a support group. Knowing that others understand and empathize with your struggles can alleviate the sense of isolation that often accompanies OCD.

Case Study: Community Support and Shared Recovery

Consider the experience of Sarah, a freelance writer who had long felt isolated by her OCD. When Sarah began CBT, she also joined an online community for women battling similar challenges. In this supportive environment, Sarah was able to share her successes and setbacks, gaining insights from others who had navigated similar hurdles. The encouragement she received from this community reinforced her commitment to CBT and helped her view her progress in a more positive light. Sarah's story illustrates that while CBT provides the tools for recovery, a supportive network helps sustain long-term change.

The Road Ahead: A Commitment to Continuous Growth

CBT is not a one-time intervention but a lifelong commitment to growth and self-care. As you integrate CBT techniques into your daily life, remember that setbacks are a natural part of the recovery process. Each challenge encountered offers an opportunity to refine your strategies and deepen your resilience. Over time, the obsessive thoughts and compulsive behaviors that once defined your experience will lose their power, allowing you to lead a life enriched by clarity, balance, and self-compassion.

Looking to the Future

As you continue your journey, consider revisiting resources such as Brain Lock, When in Doubt, Do Nothing, and The Mindfulness Solution for Anxiety for additional insights and inspiration. These works offer valuable perspectives and practical tools that can complement your CBT practice and support your ongoing recovery.

This chapter has provided an introduction to Cognitive-Behavioral Therapy as the gateway to reclaiming your life from OCD. Through understanding the mechanisms of CBT—cognitive restructuring, exposure and response prevention, behavioral experiments, and mindfulness—you are now equipped with a powerful toolkit to challenge and transform the thought patterns that have long governed your experience.

The stories of Rebecca, Laura, and Sarah demonstrate that recovery is not only possible but also a journey marked by resilience, growth, and the unwavering belief in your ability to change. As you incorporate the strategies discussed here into your daily routine, remember that each small step forward is a victory against OCD. Embrace the process with patience, self-compassion, and a commitment to continuous improvement.

Welcome to the road to recovery—a path illuminated by evidence-based practices, supported by professional guidance, and enriched by the collective strength of a community that understands your struggles. The journey may be challenging, but it is also a profound opportunity to rediscover yourself, free from the grip of OCD.

9

Step-by-Step: Crafting Your Personal CBT Plan

The journey toward overcoming OCD is deeply personal and uniquely challenging for every individual. In this chapter, we'll shift the focus from general strategies to a tailored, step-by-step plan for integrating Cognitive-Behavioral Therapy (CBT) into your daily life. By crafting your personal CBT plan, you not only gain a clearer understanding of the mechanisms that drive your OCD but also empower yourself with practical tools to challenge and transform those thought patterns. Drawing on insights from seminal works like Brain Lock, The OCD Workbook, and When in Doubt, Do Nothing, and enriched by real-life case studies, this chapter serves as both a roadmap and an inspirational guide toward lasting recovery.

Understanding the Need for a Personalized Plan

CBT is effective because it targets the cognitive distortions and behavioral patterns that fuel OCD. However, no two individuals experience OCD in the same way. Your personal CBT plan must be designed to reflect your specific triggers, thought processes, and daily routines. As noted in *The OCD Workbook* by Bruce Hyman and Cherry Pedrick, the most successful interventions are those that are customized to address the nuances of your experience.

A personalized plan allows you to:

- **Identify specific triggers** that set off obsessive thoughts and compulsions.
- **Pinpoint cognitive distortions** that magnify your anxiety.
- **Develop manageable exposure exercises** that gradually reduce the intensity of your fears.
- **Monitor your progress** through consistent reflection and adjustment of techniques.

Step 1: Self-Assessment and Identification of Triggers

The first step in crafting your plan is to gain a thorough understanding of your OCD symptoms. Begin with a detailed self-assessment. Keep a daily log or journal where you note:

- **Situations or thoughts** that trigger anxiety.
- **Emotional responses** and physical sensations that follow these triggers.
- **Any behaviors or mental rituals** you engage in to relieve the anxiety.

For example, consider the case of Melissa, a 29-year-old graphic designer. Melissa discovered that her anxiety peaked when she had to submit creative work to her team. Her journal revealed a pattern: whenever she doubted the quality of her designs, intrusive thoughts about failure and rejection surfaced, followed by a compulsive need to revise and recheck every detail. By documenting these moments, Melissa was able to identify her triggers clearly, laying the foundation for targeted interventions.

Tools for Self-Assessment

- **Thought Records:** Write down intrusive thoughts as they occur, noting the context and your emotional reaction. This tool is highlighted in *Brain Lock* as a means to interrupt the automatic chain of obsessive thinking.
- **Behavioral Journals:** Document instances when you engage in compulsive behaviors. Over time, patterns will emerge that reveal the underlying triggers.
- **Rating Scales:** Use subjective rating scales (e.g., 0–10) to measure the intensity of your anxiety in various situations. This quantification helps you gauge progress as you apply CBT techniques.

Step 2: Setting Clear, Realistic Goals

Once you have a clear picture of your triggers and thought patterns, the next step is to set specific, achievable goals. These goals should focus on reducing the intensity and frequency of OCD symptoms rather than eliminating them entirely—a perspective supported by many CBT practitioners.

Examples of Goals

- **Short-Term Goals:**
- "I will identify and write down my intrusive thought each day for one week."
- "I will engage in one exposure exercise this week, starting with a situation that causes mild anxiety."
- **Long-Term Goals:**

- "Over the next three months, I will reduce the need for mental rituals by 50%."
- "I will develop the confidence to manage triggers without seeking reassurance from others."

Rebecca's journey, mentioned in earlier chapters, demonstrates how setting small, incremental goals paved the way for larger breakthroughs. By celebrating each small victory—such as resisting a ritual or enduring a feared situation—she gradually built up the resilience necessary to challenge more entrenched behaviors.

Step 3: Cognitive Restructuring and Reframing Techniques

Cognitive restructuring is at the heart of CBT. This process involves recognizing irrational thoughts and replacing them with more balanced, realistic ones. The first part of restructuring is identifying cognitive distortions—such as all-or-nothing thinking, catastrophizing, or overgeneralization—that skew your perception.

Practical Techniques

- **Thought Challenging:**
- Write down an intrusive thought and list the evidence that supports it and, more importantly, the evidence that contradicts it. For instance, if you believe, "If I make one mistake, I am a complete failure," ask yourself: "What evidence do I have of my successes?"
- *As outlined in The OCD Workbook, this exercise can help diminish the power of irrational beliefs.*
- **Reframing:**
- Transform a negative thought into a more balanced statement. For example, change "I must get everything right or I will be judged" to

"Mistakes are part of learning, and one error does not define me."
- This practice, advocated by cognitive therapists, enables you to challenge the harsh inner critic that often drives OCD.
- **Visualization:**
- Imagine a scenario where you successfully face a trigger without resorting to compulsions. Visualizing positive outcomes can build confidence and reduce anxiety over time.

Case Study: Laura's Cognitive Restructuring

Laura, a young professional with "pure O" type OCD, used cognitive restructuring to manage her intrusive thoughts about contamination. Each time an intrusive thought arose, she would challenge it by listing evidence from past experiences where no harm occurred. Over time, she began to see that her fears were exaggerated distortions. Her progress mirrors the cognitive techniques detailed in *When in Doubt, Do Nothing*, reinforcing the idea that reframing one's thoughts is a powerful tool for recovery.

Step 4: Designing Exposure and Response Prevention (ERP) Exercises

ERP is widely regarded as the gold standard in OCD treatment. The idea is to expose yourself to triggers in a controlled manner while preventing the compulsive response. This gradual exposure weakens the connection between the obsessive thought and the anxiety-relieving behavior.

Steps for Effective ERP

1. **Create a Hierarchy of Triggers:**
2. List your triggers from least to most anxiety-provoking. Start with situations that generate mild anxiety and work your way up.
3. **Develop Exposure Tasks:**
4. For each trigger, design a specific exercise. For example, if touching doorknobs triggers intrusive thoughts of contamination, start by touching a doorknob and then resisting the urge to mentally review or wash your hands immediately.
5. **Set a Time Frame:**
6. Decide on a duration for each exposure session. Begin with short intervals and gradually increase the duration as your tolerance builds.
7. **Record and Reflect:**
8. After each exposure exercise, record your experience. Note any reduction in anxiety over time, which reinforces the effectiveness of the exercise.

Case Study: Marking Progress with ERP

Consider the example of Daniel—a case that illustrates ERP in action (adapted from clinical case studies). Although Daniel is not a woman, his case has parallels in how personalized ERP can be structured. Daniel's fear of contamination led him to wash his hands excessively. With the guidance of his therapist, he began a hierarchy of exposure exercises, starting with briefly touching items he deemed "safe" and gradually progressing to more challenging exposures. Over several months, his hand-washing rituals decreased significantly, proving that gradual exposure can disrupt long-standing OCD patterns. Women crafting their ERP plans can take inspiration from Daniel's systematic approach, adapting it to address the specific triggers in their lives.

Step 5: Integrating Mindfulness and Acceptance Practices

While cognitive restructuring and ERP are central to CBT, incorporating mindfulness practices can further enhance your personal plan. Mindfulness helps you observe your thoughts without judgment, reducing the immediate emotional impact of intrusive ideas. Acceptance and Commitment Therapy (ACT) techniques, as discussed in Ronald Siegel's *The Mindfulness Solution for Anxiety*, encourage you to accept your thoughts as transient mental events rather than threats.

Mindfulness Techniques to Consider

- **Daily Meditation:**
- Set aside 10–15 minutes each day for meditation. Focus on your breath, and when intrusive thoughts arise, acknowledge them without attachment.
- **Body Scan:**
- This practice involves slowly directing your attention to different parts of your body to notice sensations without judgment. It can help ground you in the present moment.
- **Mindful Journaling:**
- Combine journaling with mindfulness by reflecting on your thoughts and emotions in a non-judgmental manner. This can help you understand and accept your internal experiences.

Step 6: Building a Support System

No personal CBT plan is complete without a robust support network. Recovery is not a solitary endeavor. As you implement your plan, consider involving:

- **Therapists and Counselors:** Professionals trained in CBT can offer invaluable guidance and help adjust your plan as needed.
- **Support Groups:** Sharing your experiences with others who understand OCD can provide emotional support and practical insights.
- **Trusted Friends or Family:** Educating those close to you about your plan can foster understanding and reduce the isolation that OCD often brings.

Case Study: Community as a Catalyst for Change

Sarah, a freelance writer who struggled with intrusive thoughts, credits much of her progress to the support group she joined. In this safe space, Sarah not only shared her CBT exercises but also learned new strategies from others. The camaraderie and mutual accountability within the group were critical in keeping her motivated. Sarah's experience underscores the value of building a support network—a recommendation echoed in many recovery-oriented books.

Step 7: Monitoring Progress and Adjusting the Plan

Recovery is a dynamic process. As you work through your CBT plan, it's essential to track your progress and be willing to adjust strategies as needed. Regularly review your thought records, exposure logs, and journal entries. Celebrate small victories and be patient with setbacks. Remember, progress in CBT is often gradual, and even minor improvements are significant steps forward.

Tools for Monitoring

- **Weekly Check-Ins:**
- Dedicate time each week to reflect on your progress. Note any recurring challenges and brainstorm solutions.
- **Progress Charts:**
- Visual aids, such as graphs or charts tracking your anxiety levels over time, can provide concrete evidence of improvement.
- **Therapist Consultations:**
- Regular sessions with your therapist can help you refine your plan based on your experiences and feedback.

Bringing It All Together: Your Personal CBT Blueprint

By now, you should have gathered a suite of tools—from cognitive restructuring and ERP to mindfulness practices and support network building. Your personal CBT blueprint is not a static document but a living plan that evolves with your recovery. It serves as both a map and a diary of your progress, highlighting areas of success and those needing further attention.

Sample CBT Plan Outline

- **Self-Assessment:**
- Maintain a daily thought and behavior journal.
- Identify top five triggers and document associated emotions.
- **Goal Setting:**
- Short-Term: Engage in one mild exposure exercise per week.
- Long-Term: Decrease the frequency of compulsive behaviors by

50% in six months.
- **Cognitive Restructuring:**
- Daily practice of thought challenging and reframing exercises.
- Weekly review of cognitive distortions with a therapist.
- **ERP Protocol:**
- Create a hierarchy of triggers with specific exposure tasks.
- Set time goals for each exposure, gradually increasing difficulty.
- **Mindfulness Practices:**
- 10–15 minutes of daily meditation or body scan.
- Mindful journaling to reflect on experiences without judgment.
- **Support Network:**
- Weekly participation in a support group or online forum.
- Regular check-ins with a trusted friend or mentor.
- **Progress Monitoring:**
- Weekly self-assessments and progress chart updates.
- Monthly therapy sessions for plan adjustments.

Final Thoughts

Crafting your personal CBT plan is a courageous and transformative act. It signifies not only your commitment to overcoming OCD but also your willingness to engage actively in the process of self-healing. As you move forward, remember that your plan is unique to you—tailor it, adjust it, and refine it as you learn more about your triggers and strengths.

The resources and strategies discussed in this chapter are supported by a wealth of research and clinical practice. Books such as *Brain Lock*, *The OCD Workbook*, and *When in Doubt, Do Nothing* provide further insights and practical techniques that can enhance your personal plan. By combining these proven methods with your own insights, you are building a foundation for lasting recovery.

Recovery is not linear, and setbacks are a natural part of the process.

However, each step you take—each exposure faced, every negative thought reframed, every minute of mindfulness practiced—is a victory. Embrace these small successes and use them as motivation to continue progressing on your journey.

As you integrate this personalized CBT plan into your daily routine, you are not only challenging the grip of OCD but also reclaiming the narrative of your life. With patience, persistence, and self-compassion, you are building the tools to face uncertainty head-on and to live a life defined not by intrusive thoughts, but by resilience, growth, and hope.

Welcome to the next phase of your journey—one where your personal CBT plan becomes a trusted ally in the ongoing pursuit of mental freedom and self-discovery.

10

Breaking the Cycle – Exposure and Response Prevention in Action

Exposure and Response Prevention (ERP) is widely recognized as one of the most effective methods for breaking the grip of OCD. In this chapter, we delve deeply into how ERP works in practice, explore its transformative potential through detailed case studies, and discuss how it can be integrated into your daily life. Drawing on insights from seminal works such as Brain Lock by Jeffrey Schwartz and When in Doubt, Do Nothing by Reid Wilson, this chapter provides a comprehensive, step-by-step guide to using ERP to disrupt the cycle of obsessive thoughts and compulsive behaviors.

Understanding the ERP Process

At its core, ERP is built on two key components:

- **Exposure:** Facing the thoughts, images, objects, or situations that trigger anxiety.
- **Response Prevention:** Resisting the urge to perform the compulsive behaviors or mental rituals that temporarily reduce that anxiety.

This process is based on the idea that anxiety naturally decreases over time if it is not reinforced by compulsive behavior. When you repeatedly face your triggers without resorting to rituals, the brain learns that the feared outcome does not occur—and the intensity of the anxiety diminishes.

Jeffrey Schwartz, in *Brain Lock*, explains that the "locking" of obsessive thoughts and compulsions is not a sign of weakness but a misfiring in the brain's circuitry. ERP helps "unlock" this circuit by retraining the brain to see anxiety as manageable and transient. Reid Wilson's *When in Doubt, Do Nothing* further emphasizes that refraining from immediate ritualistic responses can dramatically reduce the cycle of fear and anxiety over time.

The Rationale Behind ERP

ERP works by challenging two fundamental aspects of OCD:

1. **Overestimation of Threat:** Individuals with OCD often exaggerate the danger associated with their intrusive thoughts or situations. By confronting these fears directly, you begin to see that the outcomes are rarely as catastrophic as imagined.
2. **Reliance on Compulsions:** Compulsions, whether they are physical rituals or mental checks, provide only temporary relief. ERP teaches that this relief is short-lived and that avoiding rituals leads to long-term reduction in anxiety.

Designing Your ERP Program

Step 1: Identifying Your Triggers

The first step in an effective ERP program is to create a detailed list of your triggers. These are the thoughts, situations, or objects that spark obsessive fear or anxiety. For instance, someone with contamination fears might list public doorknobs, handrails, or even the idea of touching money. Others might identify abstract triggers such as intrusive thoughts about harm or moral violations.

Case Study – Jenna's Trigger List:

Jenna, a 32-year-old administrative assistant, struggled with intrusive fears about contamination. Over time, she compiled a detailed list that included specific locations (e.g., office break room, public transportation), specific objects (e.g., elevator buttons), and even specific times of day when her anxiety spiked. By quantifying her fear on a scale from 0 to 10, she was able to create a hierarchy of triggers, beginning with those that induced mild anxiety (a rating of 3 or 4) and progressing to those that were most overwhelming.

Step 2: Creating a Hierarchy of Exposures

Once triggers are identified, the next step is to rank them from least to most anxiety-provoking. This hierarchy will guide the gradual progression of your exposures. Starting with the less challenging triggers builds confidence and allows you to develop coping skills before confronting the most feared situations.

Reference Insight:

In *When in Doubt, Do Nothing*, Reid Wilson outlines the importance of incremental progress. He advises that the exposure tasks should be "just hard enough" to elicit anxiety without being so overwhelming that they cause complete shutdown. This balanced approach is key to sustained progress.

Step 3: Planning Specific Exposure Tasks

For each trigger on your hierarchy, design an exposure task that you can perform in a controlled setting. For example, if touching public surfaces causes anxiety, your exposure might involve touching a door handle and then delaying any mental or physical ritual for a predetermined amount of time. It is essential that each exposure is well-defined and measurable.

Case Study – Mark's Gradual Exposure:
Mark, a 40-year-old teacher, had OCD centered around intrusive thoughts of causing harm by leaving the stove on. He began with a simple exposure: turning the stove on for a minute, then resisting the urge to check it repeatedly. With his therapist's guidance, Mark gradually increased the duration of the exposure until he could leave the kitchen without engaging in his ritual. Mark's methodical, step-by-step approach is a classic example of how ERP can lead to lasting change.

Step 4: Implementing Response Prevention

The "response prevention" part of ERP is about deliberately not engaging in the compulsions that follow the exposure. This step can be the most challenging because the immediate relief provided by the compulsion is hard to resist. However, every time you refrain from performing the ritual, you are sending a powerful message to your brain—that the feared outcome is not occurring, and that anxiety can be tolerated.

Practical Tip:
Use a timer during exposures to mark the period in which you must refrain from rituals. Gradually extend the duration as you become more comfortable with the discomfort. Over time, you will notice that the urge to perform the ritual diminishes, a phenomenon known as

"habituation."

Step 5: Reflecting and Adjusting

After each exposure session, take time to reflect on the experience. Keep a journal where you record:

- The trigger and exposure task.
- Your level of anxiety before, during, and after the exposure.
- Any thoughts or feelings that surfaced.
- Whether you were able to refrain from performing the compulsion.
- Insights or observations that might help refine future exposures.

Case Study – Linda's Reflective Journal:

Linda, a 27-year-old graduate student with intrusive thoughts related to making mistakes, maintained a detailed journal throughout her ERP journey. Over several months, she noted that her anxiety levels decreased progressively with each exposure. Her journal entries revealed that the initial discomfort gave way to a sense of empowerment. By revisiting her progress, Linda was able to adjust her exposure hierarchy—sometimes returning to earlier tasks to consolidate gains before advancing to more challenging exposures.

Overcoming Common Challenges in ERP

The Urge to "Undo" the Exposure

It is natural to experience the urge to "undo" an exposure by performing a ritual immediately after facing a trigger. This reaction is deeply ingrained in the OCD cycle. Recognizing this urge as part of the process and resisting it is crucial. Over time, the need to "undo" the anxiety diminishes as your brain learns that the feared consequences do not materialize.

Dealing with Setbacks

Setbacks are an inevitable part of the recovery process. You may find that some exposures feel more difficult on certain days, or that anxiety spikes unexpectedly. It is important to view these moments not as failures but as opportunities for further learning. Revisiting techniques from *Brain Lock* can provide reassurance that setbacks are common and that persistent practice is key to long-term success.

Seeking Professional Support

While many individuals can implement ERP techniques on their own, professional guidance can be invaluable, especially when facing particularly challenging exposures. Therapists trained in CBT can provide tailored strategies, help adjust your hierarchy, and offer support when progress seems stalled.

Reference Insight:

Clinical studies and the experiences shared in *The OCD Workbook* underscore that collaboration with a therapist often accelerates the ERP process. Professional support provides structure and accountability, making it easier to push through discomfort.

Integrating ERP with Other CBT Techniques

ERP does not work in isolation; it is most effective when combined with other CBT strategies. Cognitive restructuring, for example, complements ERP by helping you challenge and reframe the irrational thoughts that trigger your anxiety. Together, these techniques form a comprehensive approach that addresses both the cognitive and behavioral aspects of OCD.

Combining Cognitive Restructuring with ERP

Before initiating an exposure, you might benefit from cognitive restructuring exercises. For instance, if you have an intrusive thought such as "I will lose control if I don't check the stove," first challenge this thought by listing evidence to the contrary. Once you have reframed the thought, proceed with the exposure without performing the checking ritual.

Case Study – Olivia's Integrated Approach:

Olivia, a 36-year-old accountant, struggled with an obsession about leaving appliances on. Before each ERP session, she spent a few minutes challenging her catastrophic thoughts about potential harm. This cognitive preparation helped her approach the exposure with a calmer mindset. Over time, Olivia found that the combination of cognitive restructuring and ERP led to more rapid reductions in anxiety. Her integrated approach is well-documented in cognitive-behavioral literature and serves as an example of how blending techniques can yield better results.

The Long-Term Benefits of ERP

The benefits of ERP extend far beyond the immediate reduction of anxiety. As you continue to practice ERP, you will likely notice a broader improvement in your overall quality of life:

- **Increased Tolerance for Uncertainty:**
- Regular exposure to anxiety-provoking situations helps you build resilience. You learn that uncertainty is a part of life and that you are capable of managing it without resorting to compulsions.

- **Enhanced Self-Confidence:**
- Successfully facing your fears—time and again—can transform your self-image. Every exposure that you complete without performing a ritual reinforces the belief that you are stronger than your OCD.
- **Improved Emotional Regulation:**
- Over time, ERP helps you become more adept at managing your emotional responses. Instead of being overwhelmed by intrusive thoughts, you learn to observe them without judgment, paving the way for more balanced emotional responses.
- **A Foundation for Other Areas of Growth:**
- The skills you develop through ERP, such as mindfulness, cognitive restructuring, and distress tolerance, are transferable to many other areas of life. This enhanced coping repertoire can lead to improvements in relationships, professional performance, and overall well-being.

Continuing Your ERP Journey

ERP is not a one-time intervention but a lifelong practice. As you gain mastery over your triggers, you might still experience occasional setbacks or periods of increased anxiety. The key is to view ERP as a flexible tool—one that you can return to whenever needed.

Reference Insight:

Books such as *When in Doubt, Do Nothing* remind us that recovery is a journey with ups and downs. The long-term practice of ERP, combined with ongoing cognitive-behavioral techniques, supports lasting change. Even when progress seems slow, the cumulative effect of repeated exposures gradually weakens the grip of OCD.

Conclusion

Exposure and Response Prevention is a powerful technique that enables you to break free from the cycle of OCD by confronting your fears and resisting compulsions. By designing a structured ERP program—beginning with identifying triggers, creating a hierarchy of exposures, and systematically resisting compulsive behaviors—you can retrain your brain to view anxiety as manageable rather than catastrophic.

Through detailed case studies such as those of Jenna, Mark, Linda, and Olivia, we see that ERP is not only effective but also transformative. These real-life examples, along with the principles outlined in *Brain Lock* and *When in Doubt, Do Nothing*, provide compelling evidence that with persistence, the cycle of intrusive thoughts and compulsions can be broken.

Remember, the journey toward recovery is gradual. Each exposure you face and each moment you resist the urge to perform a ritual is a victory—a step closer to a life where OCD no longer dictates your thoughts or actions. As you integrate ERP with other CBT techniques and build on your personal progress, you lay the foundation for increased self-confidence, emotional resilience, and a more fulfilling life.

Welcome to the ongoing journey of recovery—a journey marked by courage, persistence, and the promise that every challenge overcome through ERP brings you closer to mental freedom and lasting change.

11

Sustaining Recovery – Building Resilience and Self-Care Routines

The battle against OCD does not end with a reduction in compulsive behaviors or intrusive thoughts. Recovery is a long-term process that involves building resilience, nurturing self-care, and maintaining the gains made through therapy. In this chapter, we explore strategies for sustaining recovery, preventing relapse, and creating a lifestyle that supports mental well-being. Drawing on insights from works like The Mindfulness Solution for Anxiety by Ronald Siegel and The OCD Workbook by Bruce Hyman and Cherry Pedrick, as well as real-life case studies, this chapter provides a comprehensive guide to integrating self-care routines and resilience-building practices into everyday life.

The Importance of Sustaining Recovery

After months—or even years—of dedicated therapy, it can be tempting to view recovery as a destination. However, maintaining progress is an ongoing journey. OCD, like many mental health challenges, can ebb and flow. Stress, life changes, or even unexpected triggers may occasionally cause symptoms to resurface. Recognizing that relapse is not a sign of failure but a natural part of the recovery process is essential. By building resilience and integrating self-care strategies, you can create a buffer against setbacks and ensure that you continue moving forward.

Viewing Recovery as a Lifestyle

The concept of recovery extends beyond the confines of therapy sessions. It encompasses the lifestyle choices you make daily—your routines, your relationships, and your attitudes toward self-care. Books like *The Mindfulness Solution for Anxiety* emphasize that cultivating mindfulness and self-compassion are not temporary fixes but lifelong practices. When you approach recovery as a lifestyle, every moment becomes an opportunity to reinforce the positive changes you have worked hard to achieve.

Building Resilience: Strategies and Techniques

Resilience is the capacity to bounce back from stress, adversity, or relapse. For those with OCD, building resilience involves developing tools that allow you to face challenges without reverting to old patterns of compulsions and obsessive thoughts. Here are several strategies to help foster resilience:

1. Mindfulness and Meditation

Mindfulness practices form a cornerstone of resilience-building. Regular mindfulness meditation can help you observe your thoughts and emotions without judgment, reducing the intensity of anxiety and creating a sense of inner calm.

- **Daily Meditation:** Set aside 10–15 minutes each day for mindfulness

meditation. Apps like Headspace or Insight Timer can guide you through practices that focus on breathing, body scans, or simply observing your thoughts.
- **Mindful Breaks:** Throughout the day, take short breaks to practice deep breathing or engage in a brief mindfulness exercise. These pauses can help you manage stress and maintain emotional balance.

2. Physical Self-Care

Physical well-being and mental health are deeply interconnected. Regular exercise, proper nutrition, and sufficient sleep can all bolster resilience and reduce the likelihood of relapse.

- **Exercise:** Engaging in regular physical activity releases endorphins, which can improve mood and reduce anxiety. Whether it's a brisk walk, yoga, or more vigorous exercise, find a routine that suits you.
- **Nutrition:** A balanced diet supports overall health and can influence mood and energy levels. Consider consulting with a nutritionist if you have specific dietary concerns.
- **Sleep Hygiene:** Prioritize good sleep habits—establish a consistent sleep schedule, create a calming bedtime routine, and ensure your sleep environment is conducive to rest.

3. Cognitive Strategies

Maintaining progress in CBT involves continuing to challenge negative thoughts and cognitive distortions.

- **Thought Journaling:** Keep a daily journal where you record intrusive thoughts, your emotional responses, and any progress you make. Reflecting on these entries can help you identify patterns and

celebrate improvements.
- **Cognitive Restructuring:** Continue to practice reframing techniques. When you catch yourself in a cycle of all-or-nothing thinking or catastrophizing, pause and ask, "What is the evidence for this thought? How might I reframe this situation more realistically?"
- **Behavioral Experiments:** Periodically test your assumptions by engaging in controlled experiments. For instance, if you're afraid that skipping a minor ritual will lead to catastrophe, try it in a low-stakes situation and observe the outcome.

4. Emotional Regulation

Learning to manage emotions effectively is key to sustaining recovery.

- **Mindfulness-Based Stress Reduction (MBSR):** Programs like MBSR teach techniques for managing stress through meditation, body awareness, and gentle yoga. These techniques can help reduce the emotional intensity associated with OCD triggers.
- **Self-Compassion:** Embrace practices that encourage self-kindness. As Brené Brown highlights in *Daring Greatly*, vulnerability and self-compassion are essential for emotional healing. Consider exercises like writing a compassionate letter to yourself or practicing affirmations that reinforce your worth regardless of perfection.

Creating a Sustainable Self-Care Routine

A sustainable self-care routine is not about indulgence or luxury; it's about consistently prioritizing your well-being. A well-rounded self-care routine integrates mental, physical, and emotional strategies that reinforce the progress made in therapy.

Structuring Your Day

Designing a daily schedule that includes time for work, leisure, and self-care is a powerful way to sustain recovery.

- **Morning Rituals:** Start your day with a routine that sets a positive tone. This might include meditation, a healthy breakfast, and a brief review of your goals.
- **Scheduled Breaks:** Incorporate regular breaks into your day to check in with yourself. A five-minute pause every hour can help you manage stress and prevent burnout.
- **Evening Reflections:** End your day by reflecting on your progress. Consider journaling about what went well, what challenged you, and what you're grateful for. This reflective practice can consolidate learning and foster a sense of accomplishment.

Engaging in Activities That Bring Joy

Recovery is bolstered when you engage in activities that nurture your spirit and bring genuine joy.

- **Hobbies and Interests:** Whether it's painting, gardening, reading, or playing music, make time for hobbies that allow you to express yourself and relax.
- **Social Connections:** Foster relationships with people who support your recovery. This may involve regular meetings with friends, participation in support groups, or engaging in community activities.
- **Creative Expression:** Creativity can be a powerful outlet for processing emotions. Consider creative writing, drawing, or any form of art that resonates with you.

Preventing Relapse: Recognizing Warning Signs and Taking Action

Even with a robust self-care routine, occasional setbacks are a natural part of recovery. The key to long-term success lies in recognizing early warning signs of relapse and taking proactive steps to address them.

Early Warning Signs

Be mindful of signals that may indicate a potential relapse:

- **Increased Anxiety:** Notice if anxiety levels start to rise consistently, especially in situations that previously caused mild discomfort.
- **Return of Rituals:** Pay attention if you begin to perform old compulsions more frequently.
- **Negative Self-Talk:** Monitor your inner dialogue. An uptick in harsh self-criticism or catastrophic thinking can signal that you're slipping back into old patterns.
- **Isolation:** Withdrawal from social interactions and support networks may indicate that you're struggling to cope.

Strategies to Prevent Relapse

- **Regular Check-Ins:**
- Schedule periodic self-assessments. Use a checklist or journal to monitor your symptoms and reflect on your emotional state. These check-ins can help you identify any worrying trends early on.
- **Maintain Therapy and Support Networks:**
- Continuing therapy—even on a less frequent basis—can provide ongoing guidance. Support groups and peer networks also serve as reminders that you are not alone in your journey.

- **Adjust Your Self-Care Routine:**
- Life changes, and so might your stressors. Be open to adapting your self-care practices as needed. This might mean adjusting your exercise routine, exploring new mindfulness techniques, or even revisiting cognitive restructuring exercises.
- **Develop a Relapse Prevention Plan:**
- Create a written plan outlining what steps to take if you notice early warning signs. This plan might include scheduling an extra therapy session, reaching out to a trusted friend, or revisiting your exposure hierarchy.

Case Study: Karen's Relapse Prevention Plan

Karen, a 37-year-old project manager, had experienced several relapses in her OCD recovery. After working with her therapist, she developed a detailed relapse prevention plan. Karen's plan included a weekly self-assessment checklist, a list of warning signs, and a schedule for additional support sessions during periods of high stress. When Karen noticed an increase in her obsessive thoughts after a stressful work project, she was able to refer back to her plan. By reaching out to her support group and scheduling an extra session with her therapist, Karen was able to address the issue before it escalated into a full relapse. Her experience highlights the importance of being prepared and proactive.

Integrating Lessons from Seminal Works

Many influential books offer guidance on sustaining recovery and building resilience. For example, in *The Mindfulness Solution for Anxiety*, Ronald Siegel outlines practical mindfulness techniques that have been shown to reduce anxiety and improve emotional regulation. Similarly, *The OCD Workbook* provides structured exercises for ongoing self-assessment and cognitive restructuring. Drawing on these resources can provide both inspiration and concrete tools to support your long-term recovery.

Inspirational Insights

- **Brené Brown's *Daring Greatly*:**
- Brown reminds us that vulnerability is not a weakness but a strength. Embracing vulnerability can lead to deeper connections with others and a more authentic self.
- **Andrew Solomon's *The Noonday Demon*:**
- Although focused more broadly on depression, Solomon's work emphasizes the importance of understanding mental illness as a complex interplay of biological, psychological, and social factors. This holistic view reinforces the need for comprehensive self-care.

Cultivating a Growth Mindset

Adopting a growth mindset—believing that you can improve with effort and persistence—is essential for sustaining recovery. Every setback, every challenge, is an opportunity to learn and adapt. Recognize that recovery is not about perfection but about continuous growth. Celebrate your progress, no matter how small, and remind yourself that each step forward strengthens your resilience.

Daily Affirmations and Reflective Practices

Incorporate practices that reinforce your growth mindset:

- **Daily Affirmations:**
- Start your day with positive affirmations such as "I am resilient," "I

am capable of overcoming challenges," or "Every step I take brings me closer to freedom."
- **Reflective Journaling:**
- At the end of each day, write down one thing you learned about yourself or one small victory. Over time, these reflections build a powerful narrative of progress and strength.

Sustaining recovery from OCD is an ongoing journey that requires a multifaceted approach. Building resilience and integrating self-care routines into your daily life not only help prevent relapse but also enrich your overall quality of life. By embracing mindfulness, physical self-care, cognitive strategies, and supportive social networks, you create a strong foundation that can carry you through the inevitable ups and downs of recovery.

Through the experiences of individuals like Melissa, Mark, Linda, Karen, and countless others documented in therapy sessions and in literature, we see that long-term recovery is achievable when supported by a comprehensive self-care routine. Resources such as *The Mindfulness Solution for Anxiety*, *The OCD Workbook*, and *Daring Greatly* provide valuable insights and practical tools that can guide you on this path.

Remember, recovery is not a destination but a dynamic process—a lifestyle of ongoing self-improvement, self-compassion, and resilience. Each day offers new opportunities to reinforce your progress and celebrate the courage it takes to live authentically, free from the constraints of OCD.

As you move forward, be patient with yourself. Embrace the small victories, learn from setbacks, and continue to adapt your self-care routines as your life evolves. With a commitment to sustaining recovery and a proactive approach to building resilience, you are well-equipped to face life's challenges and maintain the hard-won freedom from OCD.

Welcome to a future where your mental health is nurtured, your progress is celebrated, and every day is a testament to your strength and resilience.

12

Living Beyond OCD – Empowerment, Advocacy, and the Future

Recovery from OCD is not simply about reducing symptoms—it's about reclaiming your life, your voice, and your future. In this final chapter, we explore what it means to live beyond the grips of OCD. We discuss empowerment through self-advocacy, the importance of using your experiences to educate and support others, and envisioning a future defined not by the disorder, but by resilience and hope. Drawing on insights from influential works like Daring Greatly by Brené Brown, Freedom from Obsessive Compulsive Disorder by Jonathan Grayson, and Brain Lock by Jeffrey Schwartz, as well as the lived experiences of many who have navigated this journey, we offer a roadmap to transforming recovery into lifelong empowerment.

Embracing a New Identity

One of the most transformative aspects of recovery is the gradual shift from being defined by OCD to defining oneself through values, passions, and strengths. For many women, OCD has been a relentless companion—its intrusive thoughts and compulsive rituals infiltrating every aspect of life. Yet as you move toward a life of empowered recovery, you begin to see that OCD is only one part of your story.

Case Study: Rebecca's Transformation

Rebecca, a 34-year-old teacher, once felt imprisoned by intrusive thoughts that undermined her confidence both in the classroom and at home. Over the course of her recovery—bolstered by Cognitive-Behavioral Therapy (CBT) and Exposure and Response Prevention (ERP)—Rebecca learned to separate her identity from her symptoms. She began to see her struggles as a source of strength, using her journey to mentor colleagues and support other women battling similar challenges. Her transformation is reminiscent of the narrative in *Daring Greatly*, where vulnerability becomes a pathway to authentic leadership and connection.

Defining Your Core Values

Living beyond OCD starts with a deep exploration of your core values. Ask yourself: What truly matters to me? What do I want my life to represent? By reflecting on these questions, you can build a vision for your future that goes beyond the limitations imposed by OCD. Consider incorporating practices like journaling or guided meditations focused on self-discovery. Books such as *The Mindfulness Solution for Anxiety* encourage a reflective approach that helps identify what is truly essential, allowing you to design a life that honors your authentic self.

Empowerment Through Self-Advocacy

As you continue your journey, self-advocacy becomes a cornerstone of empowerment. Living with OCD means sometimes having to educate those around you—be it family, friends, or colleagues—about the realities of the disorder. Self-advocacy not only helps create a supportive environment but also reinforces your agency in managing your mental health.

Sharing Your Story

There is power in sharing your story. Personal narratives can shatter stigmas and foster a sense of community among those who might otherwise feel isolated. For example, many women have found that writing blogs, participating in podcasts, or speaking at events not only boosts their own recovery but also helps others feel seen and understood. In *Freedom from Obsessive Compulsive Disorder*, Jonathan Grayson emphasizes that the act of sharing one's experiences can transform personal suffering into a tool for communal healing.

Case Study: Maria's Advocacy

Maria, a new mother who once battled debilitating postpartum OCD, turned her struggle into a platform for advocacy. After learning to manage her intrusive thoughts with the help of therapy and support groups, she began volunteering for maternal mental health organizations and eventually became a spokesperson for mothers experiencing similar challenges. Her willingness to be vulnerable not only accelerated her own recovery but also helped countless others find hope and resources during difficult times.

Educating Others

Self-advocacy also involves educating others about OCD. Despite increased awareness, many misconceptions persist—such as the belief that OCD is merely a quirk or that those who suffer can simply "snap out of it." By sharing evidence-based information—perhaps drawing on excerpts from *Brain Lock* or *The OCD Workbook*—you can help demystify the disorder. Consider organizing workshops or support groups where experiences and research merge to create a more accurate narrative around OCD.

Setting Boundaries and Demanding Respect

Living beyond OCD means learning to set healthy boundaries in all areas of life. Whether it's at work or in personal relationships, clearly communicating your needs is essential. Assertiveness training, often recommended in CBT programs, can help you express these boundaries without guilt. When you assert your needs—such as requesting understanding during moments of vulnerability or refusing to engage in harmful behaviors—you reinforce the message that you are in control of your life.

Cultivating Resilience Through Ongoing Growth

Recovery is not a destination but a continuous process of growth. As you live beyond OCD, maintaining your well-being requires ongoing effort. This means integrating practices that bolster resilience, adapting to life's changes, and continuously reinforcing a positive, growth-oriented mindset.

Lifelong Learning and Adaptation

One of the most exciting aspects of recovery is that it opens the door to lifelong learning. Explore new hobbies, take up classes, or volunteer in areas that ignite your passion. The act of learning new skills not only distracts from intrusive thoughts but also builds confidence and fosters a sense of accomplishment. Engaging with diverse interests can lead to new social networks and opportunities that enrich your life beyond the boundaries of OCD.

Mindfulness and Meditation as Daily Practices

Mindfulness and meditation have been cited repeatedly in recovery literature as tools that promote sustained mental health. The practice of mindfulness helps keep you anchored in the present, reducing the likelihood of ruminating on past failures or worrying about future uncertainties. Daily meditation sessions—even brief ones—can serve as a reset button for your mind. Resources like *The Mindfulness Solution for Anxiety* provide guided practices that can be adapted to your lifestyle, ensuring that mindfulness remains an integral part of your daily routine.

Ongoing Therapy and Peer Support

While many individuals eventually transition away from intensive therapy, periodic check-ins with a mental health professional can be invaluable. These sessions can help you stay on track, adapt your coping strategies to new challenges, and prevent relapse. Additionally, staying connected with peer support groups can offer ongoing encouragement and accountability. Many find that a blend of professional guidance and peer support is the most effective approach to long-term recovery.

Case Study: Laura's Continued Growth

Laura, who once struggled with "pure O" type OCD, now attends monthly therapy sessions and actively participates in an online support community. These resources have helped her not only maintain her progress but also discover new interests, such as creative writing and advocacy. Laura's story illustrates that even years into recovery, there is always room for growth, learning, and new forms of self-expression.

Using Your Experience to Make a Difference

Your journey through OCD can become a powerful catalyst for change—not only in your own life but also in the lives of others. Many who have walked this path feel compelled to give back by helping those who are still in the throes of their struggles.

Advocacy in the Community

Consider ways to involve yourself in community initiatives that promote mental health awareness. This could mean joining advocacy groups, supporting mental health charities, or even working with local schools and organizations to develop educational programs on OCD and anxiety disorders. By taking an active role in advocacy, you contribute to a broader cultural shift that recognizes mental health as an essential component of overall well-being.

Mentoring and Peer Support

Mentorship is another powerful way to use your experience. By offering guidance to others who are just beginning their recovery journey, you create a ripple effect of empowerment. Many former clients of CBT and ERP programs have found that becoming a peer mentor not only reinforces their own progress but also builds a supportive network that benefits everyone involved. Books like *The OCD Stories* highlight numerous accounts where mentorship has led to significant positive outcomes for both mentor and mentee.

Writing and Speaking Out

Some find that writing a book, starting a blog, or speaking publicly about their experience can be transformative. These platforms offer a way to articulate your journey, share insights, and offer hope to others who may feel trapped by their symptoms. Whether it's through a local community event or a national conference, sharing your story can inspire change and foster understanding.

Envisioning the Future

As you look toward the future, it's important to reframe your perspective. Rather than seeing OCD as a constant shadow, envision it as a chapter in your past—a challenge that has shaped you, taught you resilience, and ultimately empowered you to live more fully. This reframing is supported by the ideas in *Daring Greatly*, which remind us that our vulnerabilities do not define us—they refine us.

Setting New Goals and Aspirations

Living beyond OCD means setting new personal and professional goals that reflect the person you are becoming. What dreams did you set aside because of your struggles? What new passions have emerged since beginning your recovery? Revisit these aspirations and set actionable steps toward achieving them. This process not only directs your focus toward positive outcomes but also reinforces your sense of purpose and agency.

Creating a Vision Board

One practical exercise is to create a vision board—a visual representation of your goals, values, and dreams. Fill it with images, quotes, and reminders of your journey, your progress, and your aspirations. This board serves as a daily reminder that you have the power to shape your future, free from the confines of OCD.

Embracing Change and Uncertainty

Part of living beyond OCD is embracing the inherent uncertainty of life. The recovery journey has taught you that while you cannot control every outcome, you can control how you respond to challenges. This perspective fosters a sense of freedom and opens up possibilities for growth. Every new experience becomes an opportunity to learn and adapt, strengthening your resilience even further.

Living beyond OCD is not about erasing the past—it's about building a future where your experiences inform your strength and your voice. It's about understanding that while OCD may have been a significant part of your journey, it does not define your entire identity. You are more than your struggles; you are a person of resilience, passion, and potential.

By embracing empowerment through self-advocacy, committing to ongoing growth, and using your experiences to make a positive impact, you create a life that transcends the limitations of OCD. The insights drawn from works such as *Brain Lock*, *Daring Greatly*, and *Freedom from Obsessive Compulsive Disorder* remind us that recovery is a dynamic, multifaceted process—one that invites you to live authentically and courageously.

Through real-life examples like those of Rebecca, Maria, Laura, and many others, we see that the journey toward mental freedom is filled with challenges, breakthroughs, and continual learning. As you move forward, remember that every step—no matter how small—is a victory worth celebrating.

Welcome to a future defined not by the shadows of OCD but by the light of your own resilience, strength, and hope. This is your time to live beyond OCD, to advocate for yourself and others, and to build a legacy of empowerment that inspires the next generation of warriors on this journey.

www.ingramcontent.com/pod-product-compliance
Lightning Source LLC
Chambersburg PA
CBHW070044230426
43661CB00005B/752